THE WEST INDIANS
PORTRAIT OF A PEOPLE

JACQUES COMPTON

Published by Hansib Publications in 2009
London & Hertfordshire

Hansib Publications Limited
P.O. Box 226, Hertford, Hertfordshire, SG14 3WY, UK

Email: info@hansib-books.com
Website: www.hansib-books.com

A catalogue record of this book is
available from the British Library

ISBN: 978-1-906190-12-5

© Jacques Compton

All rights reserved. No part of this publication may be
reproduced, stored in or introduced into a retrieval system,
or transmitted in any form, or by any means, electronic,
mechanical, photocopying, recording, or otherwise,
without the prior permission of the publisher.

Cover illustration © Giraffarte / Dreamstime.com

Printed and bound in the UK

For my sons
Jacques and Richard
and for Lorraine

"Because as from now on people are in a position
to understand us there must be no mistake
concerning our purpose."

Aimé Césaire

CONTENTS

INTRODUCTION   9

CHAPTER 1
The creation of Caribbean Society   19

CHAPTER 2
The old system crumbles
*The significance of the slave revolt in Sainte Dominique
and the War of Independence*   36

CHAPTER 3
The Literature of Revolt
The Rejection of Europe and the Concept of Negritude   65

CHAPTER 4
The Flashing Sign
The Men of Action   93

CHAPTER 5
Caliban Demands a Hearing
A Question of Identity   114

CHAPTER 6
The Descent of Black Orpheus   143

CHAPTER 7
The Final Pattern
 Creolization   159

BIBLIOGRAPHY   178

**Mais les faisant mon coeur, préservez-moi de toute haine
ne faites point de moi cet homme de haine pour qui je n'ai que haine
car pour cantonner en cette unique race
vous savez pourtant mon amour tyrannique
vous savez que ce n'est point par haine des autres races
que m'exige bêcheur de cette unique race
car ce que je veux
c'est pour la faim universelle
pour la soif universelle**

(But in so doing, my heart, preserve me from all hatred
do not make of me that man of hate for whom I have nothing but hate
for although I have set myself down in this unique race
however, you know my tyrannical love
you know that it is not because I hate other races
that I have chosen to labour for this unique race
and that what I want
is for universal hunger,
universal thirst)

Aimé Césaire – 'Cahier D'un Retour Au Pays Natal.'

Qui et quel nous sommes? Admirable question!"

Aimé Césaire

INTRODUCTION

GILBERTO FREYRE, A BRAZILIAN ANTHROPOLOGIST AND one of the finest authorities, along with Melville Herskovits, on the black people in the Western Hemisphere, has observed that the Africans who survived the Middle Passage, and arrived in the New World, were no longer Africans but West Indian Blacks who were slaves, an entirely new, an altogether different category of beings both historically and socially.

We must take that to mean that something drastic had happened to the Africans, during that voyage, that changed them so radically. To understand more fully what had happened, we must delve into History, Economics, Sociology and Anthropology.

When we look at the development of mankind we discover that all those other peoples have or had evolved from a certain primitive civilization to whatever or wherever they are to-day. When we examine in particular the relationship between Europe and Africa, after the fall of Carthage, for example, we discover that that relationship was friendly, respectful and civilized. Europe and Africa had met, once again, but as trading partners. Some kingdoms, notably that of the Congo, had established diplomatic relations with Europe and many Congolese held high office in the Church, the Army and the Civil Service both in the Congo and in Portugal during the fifteenth century.

Renaissance Europe flourished, and so did the various kingdoms in Africa. Two centuries later we discover that while in Europe Raphael and Michelangelo were painting their finest works, Shakespeare, Racine and Molière were producing some of their most laudable and accomplished pieces, and John Milton and his contemporaries sang, at that comparable stage of development in Africa, mankind there was suddenly and brutally arrested in their evolutionary development, and Africa's people were turned into merchandise, into property, demoted from persona to res, to be bought and sold just as cotton, tobacco and sugar were bought and sold.

Whatever the Africans' lifestyle, whatever philosophical outlook they had worked out for themselves during that evolutionary development, they had been forced to change all that during that voyage which has come to be known as the Middle Passage.

In the New World of the Caribbean slave society where they had arrived, they were broken, battered and moulded, until the Europeans had made of them those specific beings which were required for the express demands of slavery on the plantations in the West Indies. African ontology, African metaphysics which had been based on a very close relationship of one human being to another, had had to be altered drastically.

That is what we must take it to mean when Gilberto Freyre said that these people were no longer Africans; they were West Indian blacks who were slaves.

We must now take a look at the African-West Indian's background because that is what is important to an understanding of him. The people who were brought from Africa to the West Indies came from a variety of nations with a diversity of social, economic, political and cultural institutions. They came also from a number of kingdoms many of which were highly organized entities. In the Caribbean today we have recognized many of the vital elements of African culture which existed in the islands during the period of slavery and which have extended their influences into the present.

In those African kingdoms law and order reigned and the people were under the direction of their kings and priests. With that went a discipline which is traditional in African culture. Discipline ruled within, as well as outside the family, and that discipline was exacted from the earliest days in the life of the child. Camara Laye's *L'Enfant Noir* and René Maran's *Batouala* and several other African novels illustrate that fact. Maran was a Martiniquan, and was the first black writer to write of traditional African village life from within.

Although in those African societies there were many systems of religious beliefs, one element, however, seems to have been common to them all – the belief in Magic. Magic constituted only one aspect of those systems in which pantheons of deities, each pantheon and each member of each pantheon with its special function, were held to control the destinies of the world. Another aspect of West African culture which we recognize in certain areas of the Caribbean, is the ancestral cult with the spirits of the dead envisaged as living on in another world, yet very alert to manifest power for good or evil among their descendants.

In ceremonials the pattern of the various nations were similar: the worship of the gods through the dance, the phenomenon of possession of devotees of the deities; the place of song in worship; the specific character of the music; the use of drums and other percussion instruments in religious rites.

When we look at the political structure we see that the monarch towered above the structure of African life but that there was also a highly efficient administrative organization.

Above all, the basic attitude of the African to life was a blend of co-operation and competition, and many of the societies had a pecuniary base with women dominating the economy.

That, in brief, constitutes the cultural patterns from which most of the West Indian islands obtained those elements which have survived. West Indian culture, therefore, when it finally emerged, was inevitably Africa-based, but we shall look at that later on.

The Europeans also played their part, and that part is of vital importance. We need, therefore, when we set out to study the West Indian people, to look at the European types with which, or with whom the Blacks came into contact, and to examine the behaviour of those types that encroached upon the African habit of thought and action, and, merging with the African elements, gave shape to the present-day West Indian way of life.

It has been observed that when peoples of differing customs, beliefs and cultural heritages come into contact with each other, both give and each take. What aspects of the new cultures a given people take, and what they, in turn, give, must inevitable vary according to the particular historical situation in which that contact takes place. In the Caribbean, when Europe and the people of Africa met, in was in an atmosphere of chaos and violence; the chaos of slavery and the violence necessary to maintain the slave society during the four hundred years of its existence.

Having said that we shall look now at what was created in the West Indies – that unprecedented experiment which resulted in the creation of that unique individual made expressly for the purpose of slavery on the plantations.

First the African, that complete man in himself, had to be dehumanized. We begin, then, with the recorded account of one of the men on the spot who had been engaged in the traffic of slaves, Eannes de Azurara, a Portuguese nobleman, who has left us this graphic account:

> "On the 8th day of August 1444, very early in the morning on account of the heat, the mariners began to assemble their lighters and to disembark their captives, according to their orders. Which captives were gathered together in a field, and marvellous it was to see among them some of a rosy whiteness, fair and well made; others less white, verging on grey; others again as black as moles, as various in their complexions as in their shapes ... and what heart was so hard as not to be moved to pity by the sight of this multitude, some with bowed heads and tearful countenances, others groaning dolorously and with eyes uplifted towards heaven, as if to implore help, from the Father of all mankind; while there were others who covered their faces with their hands and flung themselves down upon the ground, and some again who gave vent to their sorrow in a dirge, after the manner of their country; and although we could not understand the words, well we appreciated the depths of their distress. And now, to aggravate their woe, men came to parcel them out into five distinct lots, to do which, they tore the son from the father, the wife from the husband, the brother from his brethren. No tie of blood or comradeship was respected; each was thrown into a place by chance."

Eannes then goes on to tell us how the Africans, thus being broken up and divided, behave:

> "embrace one another so tightly that it needs no little strength to tear them apart. Such a division indeed, was not to be effected without great trouble, since parents and children, finding themselves in different groups, would run back to each other – mothers clutched up their children and ran away with them, caring not about the blows they received so long as their little ones should not be taken from them."

The slave trade had began and with it the rapid process of the dehumanization of the Blacks, the break-up of the family as the Africans had known it. For the next three hundred years the Blacks were to continue to undergo that, and much worse: a daughter sold to a plantation in Cuba, a son to another in Barbados, the mother to a plantation in Brazil, the father to a plantation in San Domingo; nations scattered amongst the plantations in the multitude of islands throughout the Caribbean and the rest of the Americas. Soon every major Western European country was engaged in the traffic, but by the eighteenth century England had chased all the other nations off the high seas and she alone dominated the trade, supplying Blacks to the whole Western Hemisphere.

The first Englishman to venture into the slave trade was Sir John Hawkins. From the narrative of Hakluyt we read that Hawkins, after having left England in the month of October 1562, had arrived in Sierra Leone:

> *"... which place by the people of the country is called Tagarin, where he stayed some good time, and got into his possession, partly by the sworde, and partly by other meanes, to the number of 300 Negros at the least, besides other merchandise which that countrey yieldeth. With his praye he sayled over the Ocean sea unto the Island of Hispaniola and arrived first at the port of Isabella."*

Drawings and illustrations have shown us how the slaves were packed in the holds of the slave ships; within decks and in spaces which did not permit anyone to stand upright. In that manner they were transported across the Atlantic. Many died from physical maltreatment, from grief, from sheer rage and utter despair. Many must have enquired of their gods the nature of their misdemeanours which had called down upon them such horrible cruelties.

During the voyage it was customary to take the Blacks on deck once a day for some exercise, and on such occasions many took the opportunity to leap overboard only to become the victims of the sharks which were always following the slavers.

The journey might last from six weeks to two months, depending upon the weather. Haklyut in his narrative, for example, tells us that on his journey to the West Indies, Sir John Hawkins experienced some difficulties and:

> *"for the space of eighteen dayes, we were becalmed, having nowe and then contrary windes, and some Ternados, amongst the same calme, which happened to us very ill, being but reasonably watered, for so great a companie of Negros, and our selves, which pinched us all, and that which was worst, put us in such feare that many never thought to have reached to the*

Indies, without great death of Negros, and of themselves: but the Almightie God, who never suffereth his elect to perish, sent us the sixteenth of Februarie, the ordinary breeze which is the Northwest winde, which never left us, till wee came to an Island of Canybals, called Dominica."

When the weather was bad, as mentioned above, say, during a gale or a hurricane, ('Ternados'), the hatches were battened down to protect the cargo, and the Blacks were denied that daily exercise on deck. That bad weather might last a day or several days, and during that time the Blacks were kept down below in the stifling heat, eating, drinking, urinating, defecating, getting sea-sick, vomiting, dying, tempers fraying, quarreling, children being born, and dying, also, all in that one spot where they were packed and chained, having to live and sleep in all that muck and filth and stench until the storm ceased. After one such storm a doctor had to go down below to see what of the cargo was safe and how much had been lost. He has left us this account:

"Some hot and blowing weather having occasioned the portholes to be shut and the grating to be covered, fluxes and fevers among the negroes resulted. While they were in this situation, my profession requiring it, I frequently went down among them, till at length their apartments became so extremely hot as to be only sufferable for a very shirt time. But the excessive heat was not the only Thing that rendered their situation Intolerable. The deck, that is the floor of their rooms, was so covered with the Blood and mucus which had proceeded from them in consequence of the flux, that it resembled a slaughter-house. It is not in the power of the human imagination to picture a situation more dreadful and disgusting. Numbers of the slaves had fainted, they were carried on deck, where several of them died, and the rest were with difficulty restored. It nearly proved fatal to me also."

No white man would have survived down there under those conditions. Yet millions of the Blacks did survive. A hundred years later a black West Indian poet from Martinique, Aimé Césaire, looking back at his people's history, at that horrible journey across the Atlantic, the Middle Passage, tells us what he hears and sees:

INTRODUCTION 15

> *"I hear rising from the holds below the curses of the chained, the hiccups of the dying, the splash of someone thrown into the sea...the baying of a woman in labour....the scraping of fingernails seeking throats....the sneering of the whip, the scurrying of vermin across worn-out bodies ... "*

So there we have it. That's them, the West Indian blacks.

Whatever life the Africans may have lived before being taken away from Africa, from their accustomed communal societies in their respective nations, they went straight into a modern industrial society – the sugar plantations of the West Indies; a plantation society created in the West Indies by the European plantation and slave owners. They were no longer Africans; they were West Indian Blacks who were slaves, an entirely new, an altogether different historical and social category of beings. A new kind of people had been created, or fashioned, specifically for the slave society of the West Indian islands.

How were they received and treated, those Blacks who had survived the voyage and were landed in the West Indies? For one account let us go to an Englishman who was in Barbados at the time. He is Richard Ligon and he tells us that:

> *"When they are brought to us, the Planters buy them out of the ship, where they find them stark naked, and therefore cannot be deceived in any outward infirmity. They choose them as they do horses in a Market; the strongest, youthfullest, and most beautiful, yield the greatest prices. Thirty pound sterling is a price for the best man negroe; and twenty-five, twenty-six, or twenty-seven pound for a Woman; the children are at easier rates."*

For another account we have this:

> *"When the ship reached the harbour, the cargo came up on deck to be bought. Their purchasers examined them for defects, looked at the teeth, pinched the skin, sometimes tasted the perspiration to see if the slave's blood was pure and his health as good as his appearance. Some of the women affected a curiosity, the indulgence of which, with a horse, would have caused them to be kicked twenty yards across the deck. But the*

slaves had to stand it. Then in order to restore Dignity which might have been lost by too intimate an Examination, the purchaser spat in the face of the slave. Having become the property of his owner, he was branded on both sides of the breast with a hot iron. His duties were explained by an interpreter and a priest instructed him in the first principles of Christianity."

That was what happened in Saint Dominique (Haiti), as described by C. L. R. James in *The Black Jacobins*. The British and the Dutch Protestants were not concerned with Christianizing their slaves, but more of that later.

What was created in the West Indies were a people unique in the modern world. C. L. R. James affirms that there have never been any people like them in history before, nor since.

Many people have asked: How was it possible for a handful of Whites in the West Indies to keep in subjection for so long such a large number of slaves?

There was the Police Force for the day-to-day administration of Law and Order. Then there was the militia to quell any serious slave uprisings. Finally there was the Royal Navy to protect the Europeans' kith and kin and to safeguard British interests in the islands.

Richard Ligon, writing in 1640, tells us more:

"It has been accounted a strange thing, that the Negroes, being more than double the number the Christians that are there, and they accounted a bloody people, where they think they have power or advantage; and the more bloody, by how much they are more fearful than others: that these should not commit some horrid massacre upon the Christians, thereby to enfranchise themselves, and become Masters of the Island. But there are three reasons that take away this wonder; the one is, They are not suffered to touch or handle any weapons: The other, That they are held in such awe and slavery, as they are fearful to appear in any daring act; and seeing the mustering of our men, and hearing their gun-shot, (than which nothing is more terrible to them) their spirits are subjugated to so low a condition, as they dare not look up to any bold attempt. Besides these, there is a third reason, which stops all designs of that kind, and that is, They are fetched from several parts of Africa, who speak several languages, and by that means, one

of them understands not the other: For, some of them are fetch'd from Ginny and Binny, some from Cutchew, some from Angola, and some from the River Gambia."

It was a most ingenious plan, but it was not the only method which the Planters and slave owners had devised.

et le fouet disputa au bombillement des mouches la rosé sucré de nos plaies.'

(and the whip disputed with the buzzing flies for the sugary dew of our wounds)

Aimé Césaire

CHAPTER 1

The creation of Caribbean Society

WHEN SLAVERY AND THE SLAVE TRADE BEGAN, THE Europeans did not simply go to Africa, capture the Blacks, ship them to the West Indies, place them on the plantations and, whip in hand, compelled them to work. Apart from the violence and the brutality, there were a multitude of slave laws which were supposed to regulate every aspect of the slave system.

Let us begin with the Spaniards, for they were the first on the scene in the West Indies.

The Spanish treatment of the Amerindians was abominable, completely different from their treatment of the Negro slaves who came later. Yet of all the nations practicing slavery in the West Indies, the Spanish slave laws were the most lenient. The Spaniards had enacted what they called the 'Siete Partidas,' and those laws were based upon the principle that the slave was a person, 'persona' not 'res.' That meant that the slave had to receive legal protection. In the 'Partidas,' slavery was looked upon as a misfortune from whose consequences the slaves would be protected as far as possible, because the Spaniards held that the slaves were men and because "Man is a noble animal," not meant for servitude. That fact sprang from the laws of medieval Spain where there had been slavery, and that law was humane. The Spaniards simply transferred, or introduced, its principles in the West Indies. The slave master was regarded, therefore, as having duties towards his slaves as well as rights over them.

> *"A master has complete authority over his slave to dispose of them as he pleases. Nevertheless he should not kill or wound him, although he may give cause for it, except by order of the judge of his district, nor should he strike him in a way contrary to natural reason, or put him to death by starvation."*

The slave laws of the Spanish West Indies tended to favour the good treatment of the slaves and the manumitted slaves as well. The

'Siete Partidas' laid down, among other things, that the slave, in law, was entitled to the protection or intervention of the legal authorities on his behalf, and the master could actually lose his property in the slave as a result of proved maltreatment of the slave.

In certain cases of serious abuse of the slave's rights, for instance, the slave was compulsorily manumitted. Such an abuse was the violation or prostitution of a female slave by her owner.

At one time there was serious conflict between the Spaniards in Puerto Rico and the other slave-owning European powers because the Puerto Ricans were always giving asylum to fugitive slaves from the non-Spanish territories.

The Spaniards also introduced a system called the 'coartacion,' where a slave could buy his freedom after the two, master and slave, had agreed upon a price. The law stated that at no time could the master raise the price once it had been fixed. Here, again, in the West Indies, as it seemed in other things which we shall discover later, many customs started in the West Indian islands which were later exported to the rest of the colonial world. A slave, for example, was able to buy his freedom on deferred terms, that is, the slave paid the master in instalments. That law also stated that if the slave had paid the first instalment, and was then sold to another master, the slave was not required to pay more than the remainder of the original price to the new master.

As a 'coartacion,' a Spanish slave had the legal right to change his master with or without cause.

We see, then, how the relatively liberal spirit of the Spanish slave laws influenced the form of the society which sprang up in the Spanish West Indies. Let us move on now to the English.

We need to understand something about the English law with regard to property, for the basic concept of the English law in relation to the slaves was that they were property, a special kind of property, that is, property in person. Slaves, then, being merchandise when bought and sold in the ordinary course of the slave trade, once a planter had acquired a slave, that slave became the owner's property, private property, and as such, regarded in part as chattel, in part as real estate. As chattel, a slave in English law could be sold for debts. In all other instances the law of inheritance of real estate applied, and slaves could be sold or disposed of in that manner. For example, slaves could be entailed, they could be mortgaged, and they were subject to the widow's right of dower.

That was the English law then, and that is the English law to-day relating to private property, and in the days of slavery and the slave trade the English law stated that trading in slaves was a recognized legal activity.

The concept that slaves were property was thus firmly established in the laws of the British West Indian colonies. In fact, in a decree of 1677, it was held that "Negroes being bought and sold among merchants, so merchandise, also being infidels, there might be property in them."

There is something even more relevant in that respect. Certain people at the time who, apparently, did not have England's interest at heart, and who had been in the habit of smuggling a slave or two into the country in order to testify to the abominable condition of the slaves in the West Indies, and thus lend weight to the abolitionist movement, were soon put right by the distinguished authority on English law, Sir William Blackstone when he ruled that:

> "With regard to any right the master may have lawfully acquired to the perpetual service of John or Thomas, this will remain exactly in the same state or subjection for life, in England or elsewhere."

No man, then, would be allowed to tamper with another's private property, and in this instance, a man's slave.

Six years after Blackstone's ruling, another legal man handed down a different judgement. When Lord Justice Mansfield set the slave, Somerset, free, and ruled, after much prevarication, that English law did not permit slavery on English soil, the poet, Cowper, observed, in the second book of *The Task*, 'We have no slaves at home, then why abroad?" The English were crowing rather loudly about how humane they were in setting free one slave in England, while slavery was permitted and was being carried on in the British West Indies.

The appointment of a judge in England as well as in the United States of America is a political one. We are also given to understand that judges are above or beyond all political pressures. Yet when we examine the strength of the Planter-slave-owning class in England and the West Indies, and the weight of their economic arguments during those days of slavery which not even the counter arguments of an economist of the stature of Adam Smith was able to repel, and when we see the power of their representation in the House of Commons and in the House of lords, we can be forgiven for assuming that political pressure was brought to bear upon Lord Mansfield after that judgement, for his judgements later on were entirely different. We shall look at two of them.

Later that same year, 1783, a vessel, the *Zong*, on a voyage from West Africa to the West Indies with a shipment of slaves, ran into difficulties when she was becalmed and water and food were running short on board. The captain, in order to save the rest of the cargo, decided to throw overboard 132 Negroes. The owners of the slaves brought an action for insurance, arguing that the loss of the slaves fell within the clause of the policy which covered them against "all perils of the sea." Lord Chief Justice Mansfield ruled that the "case of slaves was the same as if horses had been thrown overboard," and he awarded the owners damages of thirty pounds against each slave.

Again in 1785, another insurance case came before Lord Chief Justice Mansfield. In this instance Negro slaves on a British ship had mutinied and several were killed. Lord Chief Justice Mansfield ruled that the slaves who had died in the mutiny were to be paid for by the Underwriters.

Thus the principle that the slaves were property had been firmly established in English law.

In the British West Indies laws were enacted so that the police would keep the slaves in their fixed status as the legal property of their owners. The law allowed the slave owner virtually unlimited power over his property. To maintain that law it was necessary to bring in Police regulations to uphold the convention that the slave was private property. Police Regulations, therefore, were the very foundations upon which the slave society was maintained. The Police were Whites. Without that Police force it would never have been possible to have carried on the system. Those Police regulations worked in all cases against the slaves, because the blacks had been reduced to mere property. To have had it otherwise would have meant the recognition of the slaves as ordinary persons, 'personae,' and it would then have been difficult to infringe upon their liberty and freedom.

Police law, therefore, regarding the enforcement of the subordination of the slaves was of paramount concern to the Planters. Because the slave was property, a person who stole a slave was apprehended by the Police and brought before the Courts and was convicted of the felony.

The law compensated the owner of a slave who had suffered the judicial penalty of death. To carry off a slave from the islands without the owner's consent, was punishable by death. People who aided runaway slaves were arrested by the Police and punished by the Courts.

Slaves were not allowed to wander abroad without the written consent of the Police, or of the owner. Here we have the introduction of the Pass Laws which were later taken to South Africa under the system of Apartheid. Slaves were not allowed to handle firearms, to beat drums, to blow horns, to assemble together in numbers. Police regulations covered the maintenance of all those.

Slave evidence was not acceptable against a white person, and no island in the British West Indies recognized that the wilful killing of a slave was homicide. The same attitude had applied in Kenya during the Mau Mau uprisings of the 1950s, and an Englishman who had been responsible for the beating to death of six Mau Mau suspects at the Hola Camp, was later knighted when he returned to England. On the other hand a White was only fined for the killing of a slave in the British West Indies.

In the British West Indies the brutality of the law and of the Police regulations meant that the slave society had to be maintained at all costs. In so far as the slave was allowed any personality before the law, the Police regarded him chiefly, almost solely, as a potential criminal.

Even the economic activities of the slaves were under Police supervision. Slaves were often allotted plots of land to grow food for their own upkeep. In many instances the industrious slaves would grow more than was required and then sold the rest in the Sunday market which was allowed by the Police Regulations. With that money, over a number of years, a slave was able to buy his freedom. The economic activities of the freed Negroes and of the freed Mulattos, were also subject to Police Regulations.

Intimidation, repression and brutality were the methods used by the Police in the British West Indies of the slave society and since wounds, not so old, are easily re-opened, and memories die hard, anything which to-day savours of Police persecution is immediately suspect as far as the black West Indians are concerned.

Only Whites, in the British West Indies, enjoyed the privilege of trial by Jury. In 1688, for example, the white planters who framed the laws stated that Blacks:

> " ... being Brutish slaves, deserve not, from the Baseness of their Condition to be tried by the legal trial of twelve men of their peers, or Neighbourhood, which truly neither can rightly be done, as the Subjects of England are."

To the Whites in the British West Indies, humane treatment of the slaves was of secondary importance; self-preservation was their primary concern. The laws, therefore, were meant to be excessively repressive, and that was how they remained until the end of the 18th.century when the Planters were forced to make some amends in the condition of the slaves. By that time, however, with the events in Sainte Dominque well under way, the writing had long appeared on the wall.

An historian, Bryan Edwards, also a Planter and slave owner, wrote in 1801:

> "In countries where slavery is established, the leading principle on which the government is supported is fear; or a sense of that absolute coercive necessity which, leaving no choice of action, supersedes all questions of right ... "

We will now look at the French. In the beginning the French approached the whole question of slavery in a very sophisticated way.

In 1685 the metropolitan government in France drew up a Slave Code as the basis of their laws. They called it the 'Code Noir.' That Code, although it was drawn up in France, was not intended to be a Code of French Laws. The 'Code Noir' was drawn up with the West Indies specifically and firmly in mind, and solely for dealing with the problems posed by the existence of slavery in the French West Indian islands. Nonetheless its function was the same as in the British West Indies.

The difference, and one of tremendous importance between the two countries, lay in the different political traditions.

In France the monarchy had great powers both at home and abroad. The Crown retained powers of legislation in the West Indies. Britain had it differently; the power of legislation was invested by the Crown in the island legislatures, that is, the Legislative Council and the Legislative Assembly. Britain could always claim, therefore, in matters relating to the ill treatment of slaves, that that was an internal matter. Britain has always done that, in fact, whenever and wherever Whites are in control of the political institutions in any of the colonies. Rhodesia (now Zimbabwe), was a classic example. Whenever, on the other hand, there happened to be an insurrection of the slaves with which the Police were unable to cope, Britain sent in her militia and the Royal Navy to protect her kith and kin, and her financial interests. Anguilla, some years ago, was an example, when Britain sent in the militia and a battleship that was almost as big as the island. When the militia was withdrawn, Britain sent in a large white Police Force to maintain 'law and order.'

Unlike the British colonies the French 'Code Noir' insisted on religious conformity. In France French law required the same for Frenchmen. The 'Code Noir' also regulated the status and conduct of the slaves and was concerned with public security and the protection of the slaves as property as well as of persons.

It is important to remember those differences, for while we are looking at the West Indians, we must not imagine that the various islands developed in the same manner. They had the common experience of slavery, it is true, but the black man in Cuba, Puerto Rico, Antigua, Barbados, Barbuda, Saint Lucia or Trinidad, evolved socially and culturally from each other because of the different legal, political, economic and social attitudes and traditions of the people who ruled over those islands at various times.

As with Britain, however, the 'Code Noir' laid down provisions governing the slaves as property, stating when they may be sold or seized for debts, and how the master was to be compensated if the slave was executed for any capital crime. Also, how the status of the slave was legally transmitted. There the differences ended between the two countries.

There were also laws for the protection of slaves, and laws encouraging their conversion to Christianity. There were laws for the hearing and trying, and for the punishing of Masters for their cruelty to the slaves.

Those are highly significant differences which point to the two traditions – the English and the French. In English law the interference of the Crown was limited, and the law tended to foster respect for private property. With the French the powers of the Crown in the colonies were not so limited, and the Crown could interfere in matters of private property disputes, and the slave, being property, did not cease to be in his person a matter of public concern. Thus public interference in the management of slaves was therefore more taken for granted than was the case in the British West Indies.

The 'Code Noir' was therefore based on a wider acceptance of the slave as 'persona' and not 'res.' Having some legal status, therefore, the slave was subject both to protection and to punishment in matters arising from civil disobedience. His civil disabilities were clearly stated in the 'Code Noir.'

The 'Code Noir' insisted that all slaves had to be baptized in the Catholic faith. Also, that overseers on the Plantations must be Catholics. When a British or a Dutch island was captured by the French that law was then applied to the captured island. Slaves in the French islands were also to observe Sundays and religious holidays, were to be married and, if baptized, were to be buried in consecrated ground.

The British did not do that. Slaves in the British West Indies were not permitted to marry, and the early missionaries had more than their fair share of difficulties in trying to give the slaves some religious instructions. In the end they were forced to side with the Planters and become the instruments of the State. In the British West Indies, also, slaves, mulattos and Whites were buried in separate cemeteries.

The 'Code Noir' laid down that children of slaves were to take the status of their mothers. Although, however, the slaves in the French West Indies were permitted to marry, they were only allowed to do so with the consent of their masters. The 'Code Noir' also laid down that families, when sold, were not to be broken up on certain plantations such as the sugar plantations and the indigo works; slaves could not be sold except together with the estates.

Those are fundamental to an understanding of the West Indian mentality when we come to examine and to consider family structure and social attitudes in the French, Spanish and British West Indies. In the British West Indies the people are what they inherited after three hundred years of British slave rule.

Now let us consider this. Under the 'Code Noir' slaves were tried by judges when they committed any capital offence, and the slaves had the right of appeal to the Council "the process to be carried on with the same formalities as in the case of free persons."

All this will help us to understand, or at least give us some idea of the British, French and often White West Indian's attitude to law and authority, and to the Police. It will also assist us in our understanding of the West Indian's distrust of administration officials. Whenever or wherever the West Indian smells injustice, he will be on the warpath, for injustice, violence and repression were what he had come to know exceedingly well from the Whites for three hundred years.

In 1686, one of the most touchy of questions in the West Indies, that of the admissibility of slave evidence in Court and in Police proceedings, was dealt with firmly in the 'Code Noir.' The 'Code Noir' made that evidence admissible. The slave could now make complaints against his master in cases where the master failed in his duties to the slave; for example, in the matter of his subsistence, which had always been a subject of serious complaints from slaves, and in the matter of cruel treatment. Slave masters throughout the centuries had always tried to spend as little as possible on the slaves' subsistence, and this had been a severe bone of contention between masters and slaves in the islands.

On the question of manumission, the French again were very different from the British. Before the 'Code Noir' was drawn up it was customary for the Frenchmen to free their children by the slave women the moment the children were born. The French, being Catholics, and the law concerning religious conformity and religious discipline being very strict, Metropolitan France seemed bent upon discouraging concubinage, a practice widespread throughout the Caribbean of the slave era. The 'Code Noir' laid down that the children would only be free if the parents marry, or when they married. The Frenchmen in the islands said "No!" They wished to have their children by the slave women freed immediately the children were born. That was how they had always had it, and that was how they wished it to continue. In the end Metropolitan France gave in on that point.

This vital point cannot be stressed too much when we come to consider the social and psychological development of the West Indians in the two traditions – the French and the British. The father was prepared to recognize his children, whether he was married or not to the mother, and he insisted that the law recognize the children's rights as well.

That was not the case in the British West Indies. If the English father so wished, then he freed the child. If the children were by an overseer who was often either an English, Scots or Irish indentured labourer, then that overseer had to purchase that child's freedom from the slave owner or plantation owner; that is, if the father cared sufficiently for the child. The practice more often than not was to sell the child of mixed blood (mulatto) at a higher price because of its lighter complexion, a complexion that was more acceptable to the Whites, and to make the child a house slave rather than a field slave.

There began the consciousness of colour shades in the West Indies. Here, also, was the beginning of the West Indian Middle Class about which the late C. L. R. James had a great deal to say that was not complimentary.

The 'Code Noir' laid down that once a slave was manumitted he was to be treated as a free-born subject of the monarch so long as the manumitted slave lived in obedience to the law and performed the duties of the subject.

In one respect, though, French law was less acceptable than that of the British. An English judge had ruled that English law did not permit slavery on English soil, so that from that time onwards, once a slave had set foot in England, he was free. Except, of course, if that slave were unmindful enough to return to the West Indies. Another judge, Judge Stowell, had made that painfully clear when a female slave, Grace, had returned to Antigua.

In France that was not the case. If the Black were not a freed person, black or mulatto, then he remained a slave and private property. Moreau de St. Mery, in his study of French law, states that that had not always been the practice, but that the Crown had altered that section of the 'Code Noir' in order to protect the French West Indian Planter's property.

Things did not remain as good as that for the French West Indian slaves. Both C. L. R. James and Dr. Eric Williams have pointed out why that came about. It would appear that the French middle class, that is, the merchant class, was getting more and more involved in politics. They began to agitate for laws to restrict the capabilities of the slaves, and of the freed people of colour who were in economic competition with them. The Planters were in debt to the merchants in France, just as those in the British West Indies were heavily in debt to the merchant bankers in London. The merchants began to argue that slavery had been instituted for mercantile purposes and that their commercial interests and investments had to be protected from the Blacks, and from the mulattos who were in open competition with them as freed people.

Worse, when Napoleon came to power things really began to get grim. Napoleon was an outright racialist, although he had married a mulatto woman, Josephine, formerly the Countess Beauharnais. Napoleon's attitude towards the people of colour was, however, ambiguous; he supported slavery and he wished it to be restored when the Blacks in Sainte Dominique had rebelled. Yet he had freed Blacks and Mulattos in his army, some of whom, like Alexandre Dumas (father of Alexandre Dumas, the popular novelist), held high office. Some of Dumas's admirers have argued that the only reason Napoleon did not give Dumas the Field Marshall's baton was the fact of his colour. Dumas, therefore, remained only a general. There were freed Blacks and freed Mulattos as well in the National Assembly in Paris long before, and even in Napoleon's time. Napoleon was ambitious; he needed money and he sought status, no doubt because he was of peasant stock. Josephine was beautiful; she had money; she had status for she was the widow of a Count.

The merchants and Planters in the West Indies, and in France and Britain, did not see, or they refused to see, that by increasing the pressure on the slaves to maintain their subjection, they were asking for trouble. As the economic profit from the slave plantations began to pour into Europe, the merchants and Planters argued and insisted more and more that under no circumstances must the slave system be destroyed. Any insurrection, therefore, called for punishment more severe than formerly. We read a declaration from the Crown which says that:

> *"While the slaves should be maintained and favourably treated by their Masters, the necessary precautions should also be taken to contain them within the bounds of their duty, and to prevent all that might be feared from them."*

Later we come upon a number of instructions from the Crown to its officials which state that:

> *"It is only by leaving to the Masters a power that is nearly absolute, that it will be possible to keep so large a number of men in that state of submission which is made necessary by their numerical superiority over the whites."*

Police regulations came more and more into line with those of the British and the Dutch. The duty of the Police was to see that slavery continued; that the society was kept intact, a society both in the West Indies and in Europe, whose very foundation rested upon slavery and the slave plantation economy. We see that clearly dramatized in Jane Austen's novel, *Mansfield Park*.

There are records of innumerable slave uprisings down the length and breadth of the West Indian islands and those were always quelled with the most brutal of repressions. The first slave uprising occurred in Barbados in the seventeenth century, but the most famous came in Sainte Dominique in the eighteenth century.

Barbados was the only island not stumbled upon by Christopher Columbus. It does not lie in the path of the Trade Winds, so Columbus missed it. A man named John Powell, on a voyage from Brazil to England with a shipment of tobacco, came upon the island. He returned a year later with some twelve hundred adventurers – Scots and English – and took possession of the island. What was even more ideal for them was that the island was uninhabited, the only uninhabited island in the Caribbean.

The new arrivals settled on the island and lived in relative comfort for a time, until they decided to introduce Negro slavery for they had seen that the other islands were doing well on slavery, in particular, the country of Brazil. They also introduced a large number of indentured labourers – Irish, Scots and English. Ten years after they had introduced the first slaves we get the first uprising. Richard Ligon, who has recorded the event, informs us that before the Blacks were introduced there were 11,000 people on the island. That was the population in 1620. What happened in Barbados is critical to a proper understanding of the whole three hundred years of West Indian history and what was to follow after emancipation.

> *"A little before I came thence, there was such a combination amongst them, as the like was never seen before. Their sufferings being grown to a great height, and their daily complainings to one another (of the intolerable burdens they labour'd under) being spread throughout the island; at the last some amongst them, whose spirits were not able to endure slavery resolved to break through it, or die in the act; and so conspired with some others of their acquaintance, whose sufferings were equal, if not above theirs; and their spirits no way inferior, resolved to draw as many of the discontented party into the plot, as possible they could; and those of their perswasion, were the greatest number of servants in the island. So that a day was appointed to fall upon their Masters, and cut their throats, and by that means, to make themselves not only freemen, but Masters of the Island."*

That is what happened in Barbados in 1640. That is also what happened in Mexico, Venezuela, Brazil, Guyana, Saint Lucia, St. Vincent, Grenada, Jamaica; the pattern was the same. That is what happened in Sainte Dominique in 1791; that is what happened in Cuba in 1958.

That was the beginning of West Indian history. Those West Indians, black slaves as well as indentured labourers, wanted, not only their freedom, but they wished to remove their masters and to make themselves masters of the island. In Saint Dominique the Blacks succeeded.

C. L. R. James has repeatedly pointed out that that is a characteristic of West Indian history. When West Indians reach a certain stage they want to make a change. Liberty means something to them that is completely different from other peoples' conception of it. Indeed, when we look at African history, we see that some Africans in Africa knew slavery; but that was slavery of another sort. They were people captured in war and they became integrated into their new society and made their contributions to that society. When they were taken to the West Indies they went straight into a modern industrial society – the sugar plantations, and there they saw that to be a slave was the result of their being black.

The goods they produced were not for their benefit nor for their consumption, but for someone else far away. The West Indian Blacks could not, could never, get themselves used to that kind of slavery. That is why, throughout the history of the West Indies, C. L. R. James asserts, we find that dominant desire, however expressed, but always there, that desire for Liberty; the ridding themselves of that particular burden which is the special inheritance of the black skin.

That is why, also, the West Indians have been the most rebellious people in the history of the world. They cannot stomach injustice and will fight it in whatever form it comes. The West Indians cannot be understood if that is not known. It must be understood, also, that because they were black people, they were made slaves, and the white people in the West Indies were never slaves in the ordinary sense of the word. That, too, is West Indian history.

The uprising in Barbados failed, and Richard Ligon tells us why:

> *"And so closely was the plot carried, as no discovery was made, till the day before they were put in act. And then one of them, either by the failing of his courage, or some new*

obligation from the love of his Master, revealed this long plotted conspiracy; and so by This timely advertisement, the Masters were saved. Justice Hethersall (whose servant this was) sending letters to all his Friends, and they to theirs, and so to one another, till they were secured; and by examination, found out the greatest part of them; whereof eighteen of the principal men in the conspiracy, and they the first leaders and contrivers of the plot, were put to death, for example to the rest. And the reason why they made example of so many, was, they found these so haughty in their resolutions, and so incorrigible, as they were like enough to become Actors in a second plot, and so they thought good to secure them, and for the rest, to have a special eye over them."

This must not be passed over too lightly, that observation of Ligon's concerning the slaves' incorrigibility. The Whites had seen that the slaves were absolutely determined not to give way in the slightest degree, so they had to execute them, because that was the only way that their masters could feel at all secure for the future. That is West Indian history.

Father Jean Baptiste Labat, a Jesuit priest who visited Barbados in 1700, while on his way to Grenada to look over the Church's plantations on the island, has left us an even more remarkable impression of what he saw was going on in Barbados at the time. He tells us:

"These engages are indeed numerous but should not be trusted, as they are poor Irishmen for the most part, who groan in a very harsh servitude lasting for seven or at least five years. These unfortunates are, as often as not, compelled to commence a fresh period of servitude, and no matter what protests or reasons their masters allege in order to prolong their bondages the judges never question them. Indeed if this island were attacked the masters would have their hands full, for these men would certainly turn their weapons against them, and join the invaders if only to recover their freedom. I do not mention what they would have to fear from the negroes.

The number of black slaves in the island is very great. I was told that there are more than 60,000. Again I have my doubts, but from what I observed in the leeward side, and supposing that the windward side be equally thickly populated, I can well believe that there are as many as 40,000. This is a large number for so small an island.

The English do not look after their slaves well and feed them badly. As a rule the slaves are free to work on Saturday to provide themselves all their own and their families requirements. The overseers get every once of work out of them, beat them without mercy for the least fault, and appear to care far less for the life of a negro than for a horse. It is true that they obtain their slaves very cheaply, for besides the English companies in Africa that bring over an enormous quantity of slaves to America, the interlopers bring still more slaves and sell them cheaper than the companies. The clergymen do not instruct the slaves or baptize them, and the negroes are regarded more like the beasts to whom all licence is permitted so long as they do their work properly. They are allowed to have several wives and to desert them as they please, and provided that they have plenty of children, work hard, and do not get ill, their masters are quite satisfied and ask no more of them.

The least disobedience is punished severely, and still more so are the slave uprisings. Despite these punishments, however, these risings occur frequently, for the poor wretches, pushed to extremes more often by their drunken, ignorant and cruel overseers than by their masters, at last lose patience. They will throw themselves on the man who has ill-used them and tear him to pieces, and although they are certain to receive terrible punishment they rejoice that they took vengeance on those pitiless brutes. On these occasions the English take up arms and there are massacres. The slaves who are captured are sent to prison and condemned to be passed through a cane mill, or to be burnt alive, or to be put into iron cages that prevent any movement and in which they are hung up to branches of trees and left to die of hunger and despair. The English call these tortures 'putting a man to dry.'

I admit that these tortures are cruel, but one should be careful before blaming the inhabitants of an island, no matter what nationality they be, for being frequently compelled to pass the bonds of moderation in the punishment of their slaves. For it must be remembered the objects of the punishments is to make the slaves fear and respect their masters, who would otherwise become the victims of their fury. Further that the slaves usually number two to one white man and are always ready to revolt, to risk all and to commit the most horrible crimes to gain their freedom.

These bloody executions do not happen so often among the French because our slaves are not so numerous, our religion makes them more humane, and they are treated more gently. But it was not so long ago that terrible executions took place in Martinique on account of a slave revolt that was almost general and occurred practically without any warning. It is indeed true that the desire for freedom and revenge is common to all humanity and to obtain it a man will commit any crimes."

Such an account speaks volumes. What Father Labat has described is the kind of society that was being formed in the West Indies. By the end of the eighteenth century that society was complete, and the people who formed it were the black slaves, their white masters, and the children of the white men with the black slave women, the mulattos, the people of colour, 'les gens de couleur.' It was a society founded on violence and maintained by violence.

That was the kind of society that the West Indians inherited when slavery was abolished in the islands between 1834 and 1886. Everything that the West Indians had learned about Western Christian civilization, democracy and the brotherhood of man, they had learned from the Whites, the Europeans.

'Et ce pays cria pendant des sciecles que nous sommes
des bête brutes ; que les pulsations de
l'humanité s'arretent aux portes de la negrerie ;
que nous sommes un fumier ambulant hideusement
prometteur de cannes tendres et de coton soyeux
et l'on nous marquait au fer rouge et nous dormions
dans excréments et l'on nous vendait
sur les places et l'aune de drap anglais et la viande
salée d'Irlande coûtaient moins cher que nous, et
ce pays était calme, tranquille, disant que l'esprit
de Dieu était dans nos actes.'

(And this country cried for centuries that we were
stupid brutes; that the pulsations of humanity
stopped at the doors of the slave compound;
that we are a walking dunghill, hideously promising
sweet sugar-canes and silky cotton, and they
branded us with red-hot irons and we slept in
our excrement and they sold us on the market for
less than an ell of English cloth and the salted meat
from Ireland was cheaper than us, and this country was
calm, tranquil, and convinced that
it acted in accordance with the will of God.)

Aimé Césaire

CHAPTER 2
The old system crumbles

BOTH THE LATE C. L. R. JAMES AND DR. ERIC WILLIAMS have pointed out how the fortunes of the eighteenth century had been greatly influenced by the profits from the plantation economy of the West Indies. Both Thackeray and Jane Austen were novelist of the late eighteenth and early nineteenth centuries and the gentry they portrayed in their novels, *Vanity Fair* and *Mansfield Park* respectively were able to maintain their opulent living from the proceeds of their plantations in the West Indies.

The eighteenth century was the Augustan Age of English Literature – the age of Dryden, Pope, Dr. Johnson, Addison and Steel, Swift; of Wycherley and Congreve. Dr. Johnson's servant and heir was a Black, Francis Barber, of whom Dr. Johnson once remarked that he "carried the empire of Cupid farther than most men." It was the age of the Earls of Holland when the Earls kept open house to all the intellectuals of Europe. The age of Madame de Stael and others.

England enjoyed then a life of luxury, leisure and sumptuousness that became legendary and which has never been equalled since. All that wealth which went into making England great and that life possible, came from the West Indies; the wealth created by the labour of the slaves on the plantations.

By the end of the seventeenth century England monopolised the slave trade, and in the eighteenth century the traffic she handled ran to something like 200,000 slaves a year which she supplied to her West Indian colonies and to the other nations: France, Holland, Spain, Sweden and Denmark. The cities of London, Bristol and Liverpool built their fortunes on the proceeds of the slave trade. When slavery was finally abolished in the West Indies and the Americas by 1886, the records have it that some one hundred million men, women and children had been exported from Africa and that upwards of twelve million had died during that transportation across the Atlantic.

In his opening address at the First International Conference of

Negro Writers and Artists held at the Sorbonne in Paris, from the 19th to the 22nd September, 1956, Mr. Alione Diop from Senegal, stated:

> *"The soil of Africa suffers, and is still suffering, the consequences of these cruel deportations. It is probable that if its present regrettable population position is connected with the lack of institutions designed to protect human life against natural evils, the primary responsibility for this deficiency in population rests with the slave trade. Think of the negro population which, in America and elsewhere breathes life into those countries by its labour, its democratic convictions and its creativeness. How could they have failed to enrich the economic, social and cultural life of present-day Africa, and how could they have failed to bring its density of population and its economic and cultural life up to an honourable level, and keep them there?"*

Indeed, slavery was the decisive element in the tragic destiny of the black people of Africa. Whatever progress Africa might have made during those four hundred years of slavery and the slave trade, that progress was destroyed. For just when the world was beginning to make advances mankind in Africa became merchandise, became real estate and private property. Men, women and children were bought and sold for profit, and on that profit, by the use of every devise, as Dr. Eric Williams has shown, every device of modern science and technology, began to dominate the world.

We cannot be reminded too often that in Europe Raphael painted, Luther preached, Corneille and Racine wrote, Milton sang, and Swift and Pope satirised. Through it all for four hundred years, black men, women and children were being transported across the Atlantic Ocean. For four hundred years sharks followed the slave ships for those Blacks who would be thrown overboard for one reason or another, or for those Blacks who would leap into the ocean in their vain attempt to escape. For four hundred years the West Indies and the rest of the Americas were strewn with the living and dying of a transplanted race – the black race.

Said the mulatto poet of Cuba, Nicolas Guillen : "We must learn to remember, what the clouds cannot forget."

In Europe men talked about democracy, freedom, liberty, equality and the rights of man. Yet when they looked at the West Indies they were not concerned with what was happening there. Their cry was for more slaves, more profit and for freedom in trade.

Europe had to justify what she was doing to the Africans, so they invented the theory of Race for the first time in the history of the world, so that black people became devils and imbeciles, to be consumed like tobacco, cotton, sugar and molasses were consumed, so that white people in Europe would be made whiter, purer, nobler, and, they hoped, happier.

Let us learn something more about the society which that philosophy created in the West Indies. Let us examine how that society functioned. We should do well to begin with the political structure.

From the very beginning of the creation of West Indian society, that society was based on violence and it was maintained by violence. It was also a society based on Colour and legal status. That is something that the West Indians have also inherited after the three hundred years, and more, of that system.

Politically, each island was administered independently of the other by the white Planter/Slave owning class, and each created its own separate legislatures. The existence of these separate legislatures encouraged in each island a sense of separate identity, and that narrow outlook fostered by the Whites of each island made common action impossible; made communication also impossible, so that each viewed the other in the different islands with a mixture of suspicion, envy and distaste. The Whites were concerned with the protection of their own separate interests and regarded each other with indifference, often with open hostility. Those things, that is, each island preferring to go its own way, concentrating its attention upon its own separate existence, and its own separate institutions, combined to produce that cult of political individualism and that tendency to political oligarchy which has remained so much part of the West Indies to-day,

Political individualism marked the conduct of the islands also in relation to each other, so that we found then, and still find to-day, that the lines of communication ran not from island to island, but from each separate island to the metropolitan country, either England, France, Holland or Spain, as the case may be. That is how the Whites wanted it, and that was how they created it. That was what the West Indians inherited when the Planter/Slave-owning class left the West Indies.

In that political system only Whites held power. Black slaves and Mulattos were merely property, to be represented by their white owners. Later, when the islands were administered directly from Westminster, as in the case of the British West Indies, a Father-figure was created who was supposed to know everyone and everything. That Father-figure came to be known as the Colonial Secretary, or Secretary of State for the Colonies. We now look at the economic structure and how that operated.

For three hundred years sugar dominated the economy of the West Indian islands, and the whole economic life rested upon the foundations of sugar and slavery. The growing of sugar-canes and the manufacture of sugar was an expensive business which required a large capital outlay. The English planters raised that capital in London, and the London merchants also reaped the profits. Thus the West Indian planter class found themselves able to develop their plantations, but at the same time they also found themselves chronically indebted to the merchants. They became predominantly a debtor class. On their visits to London they kept up appearances, while the slaves paid the price in hard work and persistent cruelty to induce that harder work.

In that society, also, the status of the Whites was determined by the possession of wealth, but that status, noted one historian, seemed to have demanded that that wealth be spent lavishly rather than be saved up or invested in the islands. Conspicuous consumption came to be a mark of status more valued than productive activity.

The price of a slave varied from seventy pounds for a male and sixty-three pounds for a female. Seasoned slaves and slaves bred in the islands fetched higher prices; so did the mulattos. Trained slaves, that is, the tradesmen and the artisans, fetched anything from one hundred and thirty to three hundred pounds each.

After much debate in the island legislatures, and with the blessing of the House of Commons, the Planters decided that the breeding of slaves was less expensive in the long run. It took more than two years to 'break' slaves brought over from Africa. With the children bred in captivity there was no trouble. Richard Pares, a Cambridge University scholar and economic historian, tells us about those children born into slavery that "the planter would possess them, too, without paying a penny for them."

So the stud farms were established and the slaves were encouraged to breed as many children as possible. Perhaps Father Labat did not know about the slave stud farms, but he did note that the English planters encouraged the slaves to have as many children as they possibly could. Richard Ligon also tells us that the Whites, in order to gain the loyalty of the male slaves, and to induce them to work harder, would promise them the first choice of female slaves on the arrival of fresh supplies from Africa. No doubt an over enthusiastic stud did work harder and did attach himself loyally to his master with such prospect in view.

What the stud farm meant was that a woman need not know the man who fathered her children, and the children may never come to know their father. The child, in slave law, took the status of his mother and belonged to the master of the plantation. Inevitably, after three hundred years of such a system, a way of life became established which has remained with the West Indians to this day. Slavery, we can now see, was responsible for what has now become a marked feature of West Indian family life – 'family instability'.

Even the poorest of the Whites could own slaves, although they could never afford a plantation. Several of those poor Whites would buy a slave or two, whatever they could afford, and then hire them out to the plantations, sit back and enjoy the profits. One source informs us that some planters paid from six to nine pence a day, plus food, for the hire of a slave. A valet could be hired out to visitors from Europe at eighteen shillings a month. Cooks, nursemaids, seamstresses and grooms were available for between eight and twenty pounds per annum.

Slavery, as we can see, expanded into every aspect of economic life of the islands, and that economy was never an autonomous economy, but one tied to the fortunes or misfortunes of the metropolitan country. That was the pattern then, and that is the pattern to this day; what is now known as "neo-colonialism." The people in the metropolitan countries still control the economy.

The Established Churches

We have read the views of the Jesuit priest, Father Labat; he accepted slavery. That also went for the whole of the clergy of the established churches – Catholic, Anglican and Methodist. They shared the outlook of the white ruling class with which they were closely identified by bonds of affinity and economic interests. The clergy, therefore, closed their eyes to any deviation of the Whites from the moral code laid down in their religion. They accepted slavery and regarded it as a political rather than a moral institution, and they based their work in the West Indies on an acceptance of its legality.

The directives from Europe laid down quite clearly the function of the church in the West Indies, to teach submission to the slaves and obedience to their masters. They also saw to it that the slaves broke off all cultural ties with Africa; all cultural ties, that is, not sanctioned by the church. They tried their utmost to inculcate in the slaves a sense of moral obligation which would bind them to their masters. The kind of dependency relationship which, years later, was still so marked in that of the colonizer and the colonized in Albert Memi's book, *The Colonizer And The Colonized*, a relationship which Memi says "moulded their respective characters and dictated their conduct."

By teaching submission to the slaves, therefore, the clergy was making a highly significant contribution to the maintenance of the slave system and of the slave society, for anything which strengthened the principle of subordination increased the stability of the established order. That is why some of the most virulent attacks by a number of West Indian poets have been directed against the church. That is why, also, a Haitian poet, Jacques Roumain a century after emancipation, was to vow "We shall not forgive them for they know what they do."

What neither the clergy, nor the missionaries, nor the Planters foresaw was that the slaves would soon see the contradiction inherent in the teachings of the church: the conflict of equality before the Christian god, and their enforced racial subordination.

To-day in the West Indies, where black people have accepted Christianity it is not because of, but in spite of the clergy and their racist attitude. In Africa the Africans had already arrived at their own conception of a Supreme Being who ruled by the fiat of his all-conquering will. When, therefore, they heard the clergy talk about such an omnipotent, they were already familiar with him. Where they did not reject their own African religions, as in Cuba, Haiti, Trinidad and Brazil, the African even adopted the Christian omnipotent.

The Social Structure

When, by the end of the eighteenth century, West Indian society was complete, the people who formed that society were, at the top, the Whites, at the bottom the vast majority, the Blacks, and in the middle, the Mulattos, the children of the white men with the black slave women.

What is it that held them together? What was their relationship the one with the other?

That relationship was based solely on colour and legal status. The Whites held all the power and they were backed by that proliferation of slave laws and Police regulations which we now know.

The freed people of colour, the Mulattos, did not enjoy any legal rights in the British West Indies. Neither did the slaves. The Mulattos, therefore, came to occupy a marginal position between the Whites and the Blacks. In fact, in 1802, the Mulattos had to lead a revolt before the Whites in the West Indies, and the British Parliament, would allow them the very minimum of legal rights and protection. The proliferation of criminals, prostitutes and other destitute Whites who were dumped in the West Indies every year, enjoyed more freedom than the Mulattos. About those poor Whites one observer of the period has noted that "The slave system provided them with the first means of improving their economic position." That same writer later remarked that the Whites were "very often unpolished beings, when Europe first sends them among us."

Bryans Edwards, one of the foremost historians of the slave era, and himself a plantation and slave owner, writing in 1708, tells us that:

> "The poorest white person seems to consider himself nearly on a level with the richest, and emboldened by this idea approached his employer with extended hand, and a freedom, which, in the countries of Europe, is seldom displayed by men in the lower orders of life towards their superiors. It is not difficult to trace the origin of this principle. It arises, without doubt, from the pre-eminence and distinction which are necessarily attached even to the complexion of a White Man, in a country where the complexion, generally speaking distinguishes freedom from slavery."

That racial prejudice of the Whites extended to the free coloureds as well as black slaves. John Waller, another English historian, writing in 1820, says that:

> "No property, however considerable, can ever raise a man or woman of colour, not even when combined with education, to the proper rank of a human being, in estimation of an English or a Dutch Creole. They are always kept at a respectful distance."

That sentiment was also expressed by Captain George Osborne, a character in Thackeray's novel, *Vanity Fair*. The woman in question is a wealthy mulatto from the West Indies. Osborne's father would like his son to marry her, but he steadfastly refuses to do so. "Marry that mulatto woman? ... I don't like the colour, sir ... I'm not going to marry a Hottentot Venus.".

Even in death, Blacks, Whites and Mulattos were kept separate, for each group was buried in a separate cemetery.

No one need be surprised that the West Indians have turned out to be the most rebellious people in the history of the world. They are the natural enemies of injustice. That is why, throughout their turbulent history, that dominant desire, as Richard Ligon first discovered, the desire to be free and the ridding themselves of that particular burden which is the special inheritance of the black skin. All his sufferings, all the injustices were the result of that one fact, that, being black, he was a slave, and the white man, whatever his limitations, was never a slave in the ordinary sense of the word in the West Indies.

There was one major exception, however, to that social separation of the races in the West Indies of the slave society, and that was the widespread sexual relationship between the white men and the black slave women, and later, as their numbers increased, the coloured women, the mulatto. The census in one island alone, Cuba, will be evidence enough of that widespread relationship between males and females. In 1842, the official census revealed a total population of 1,007,624 inhabitants in Cuba, made up as follows: Whites, 448,291; Mulattos or coloured, 152,838; Negro slaves, 436,495.

Throughout the history of the West Indies, many of the white men had never been able to keep their hands off the black slave women. West Indian literature, folk tales and folk songs are replete with comments and observations about that. From Jamaica to Cuba, to Trinidad and Guyana, it was the same story. Many of the Frenchmen and Spaniards married the black woman, but not the British nor the Dutch. The Portuguese, according to Henry Marsh in his book *Slavery and Race – The Story of Slavery and Its Legacy To-day* noted that the Portuguese:

> " ... showed a great dichotomy in their approach to the problem of colonisation. They conquered and maintained their colonies by force of arms. They retained their inherited sense of superiority over the local Africans. Nevertheless they accepted, perhaps more freely than any other colonising power, the practice of mixed marriages."

The British and the Dutch considered it beneath their dignity to marry a black woman, or a mulatto. Bryan Edwards, again, has this to say about it:

> *"No white man of decent appearance will condescend to give his hand in marriage to a mulatto; the very idea is shocking."*

Shocking? Yet there are numerous accounts by travellers in those days of slavery in the 15th, 16th, 17th, and 18th. Centuries, the reports of colonial officials, complaints by the clergy and ordinary lay people, all attesting to that special attraction which the black woman seem to excite in the white man. One traveller, a Frenchman, le Gentil de la Babinais, a circumnavigator, wrote a three volume book entitled *Noveau Voyage Autour du Monde*, which was published in Paris in 1728 in which he made his own observations regarding that preference of the white males for the black women. Even, he said, when there were white women available. He wrote:

> *"I have often asked him the reason for such an extraordinary taste, but they never could tell me. For my part, I believe that being suckled and reared by slave girls they derive this inclination from their milk."*

White women in the West Indies in those days never suckled nor reared their children, and left such things to the slave women.

The white men did not marry the black women, as Bryan Edwards told us. They instituted, instead, the system of concubinage which the West Indians have also inherited, white men with black or mulatto mistresses. From Martinique comes one of the finest of folk songs on that subject by a French aristocrat, Le Count DuBoulay, who wrote it in French Creole when the time came for him to leave the Caribbean and his black mistress. The song, *Adieu Foulard*.

With that knowledge of the social, political and economic background we shall now be able to appreciate the kind of society that was in existence at the time, and what was at stake in the West Indies and for the rest of Western Europe. We shall also be able to understand how, and why, one of the greatest events in the history of the West Indies came about, the successful slave revolt in Saint Dominique, the only successful slave revolt in the entire recorded history of mankind.

Above all, we shall be able to appreciate the defeat by the West Indians in Haiti between 1791-1804, of the two finest armies in the world at the time, the army of Napoleon Bonaparte and that of Britain.

Those slaves were not stupid individuals, nor were they in any way weak human beings. Richard Ligon has told us that they had to be physically fit for the stern demands of slavery. The Planters wanted only the best from Africa.

Neither did they merely dig holes to plant the sugar-canes, and then simply cut them when they were ripe. The slaves did other things as well; they ran the plantations. In his scholarly work entitled *Merchants And Planters*, Richard Pares from Cambridge University, gives us this piece of valuable information:

> *"It was not surprising that sugar was more heavily capitalised than any other plantation industry of that day. Yet we should not overrate the size nor mistake the nature of the capital required. In all the inventories which are to be found among the West Indian archives, it is very unusual for the mill, the Cauldrons, the still and the buildings to count for more than one-sixth of the total capital; in most plantations one-tenth would be nearer the mark. By far the greatest capital items were the value of the slaves and the acreage planted in canes by their previous labour. Yet, when we look closely, we find that the industrial capital required was much larger than a sixth of the total value. With the mill the boiling house and the still went an army of specialists – almost all of them slaves, but nonetheless specialists for all that. They were not only numerous but, because of their skill, they had a high value. If we add their cost to that of the instruments and machinery which they used, we find that the industrial capital of the plantation, without which it could not be a plantation at all, was probably not much less than half of its total capital."*

That tremendous economy which supported England and made her great, the greatest trading nation in the world, in fact, was made by the black slaves, many of whom were specialists. More than that, we gleam later, for many of the slaves were listed as "excellent boiler and field negro." That is, a man not only worked in the cane fields, but he did the technical work as well, specialising either as boat-builder, mason, caterer, boatswain, or boilerman. Those are the people who ran the plantations.

That is a very excellent picture of the West Indies and of the slave society, knowledge of which is of great value to us when we come to examine what happened later on. The slaves ran the plantations upon which that society depended for its existence. Above all, they were responsible for its continuance; that, had they been removed, the society would have collapsed. Hence the purpose of those brutal Police regulations and the oppressive slave laws, and the severity of the punishments meted out to anyone who tried to destroy that system upon which the society was based. In the case of England, upon which her prosperity and her greatness depended.

Again, that kind of picture of the West Indies tells us how misguided were those who had set themselves up as authorities on the West Indians – the historians, the economists, the sociologists and anthropologists, for they never told us what Richard Pares has now revealed to us. No one before had told us that the slaves had been doing all the technical work as well on the plantations, the great source of wealth of so many English aristocrats, the descendants of some of whom still own vast interests in the West Indies, and who are still drawing enormous wealth from there; the merchants in the City of London, the aristocrats of Holland House, the De Vere family, the inhabitants of Fonthill Abbey – they never told us that those plantations were run by slaves. Slave labour was not an advanced stage of labour, yet those plantations created millions, and from top to bottom, slaves ran them.

It is true that while those aristocrats of the skin were enjoying their wealth there were a few thoughtful people who were warning them that that kind of labour was not only immoral, but non-productive. One of those people was a man advanced in ideas for his time, Adam Smith. In his book *The Wealth Of Nations*, he argued against slave labour and pointed to the methods used by the French. Father Labat had made his own observations regarding the difference in treatment between France and England. Adam Smith revealed how, in one French colony, Sainte Dominique, the slaves there were out-producing, both in quantity and quality, the combined output of the British West Indian islands. No one listened. They could not hear him for the jingling of the coins in their purses.

No hope, then, of amelioration of their condition would come from the masters, so the slaves would have to do that for themselves. One man who recognised that was the French priest, the Abbé Raynal. In his book *Philosophical and Political History of the*

Establishments and Commerce of the Europeans in the Two Indies, he propounded his revolutionary doctrine, and called boldly for a slave revolt with a conviction which, to-day, some people would call fanaticism. The people did not listen to him either. In a famous passage the Abbé Raynal wrote:

> *"A courageous chief only is wanted. Where is he, that great man whom Nature owes to her vexed, oppressed and tormented children? Where is he? He will appear, doubt it not; he will come forth and raise the sacred banner of liberty. This venerable signal will gather around him the companions of his misfortunes. More impetuous than the torrents, they will everywhere leave the indelible traces of their just resentment. Everywhere people will bless the name of the hero who shall establish the rights of the human race; everywhere will they raise trophies in his honour."*

The slaves in the West Indies were eventually to make history, as the Abbé Raynal had predicted; a history that altered the fate of millions of men and the economic currents of three continents.

One man who was made a masterful study of that revolution is the West Indian historian from Trinidad and Tobago, the late C. L. R. James. From Trinidad and Tobago also came the other historians and political writers, the late Dr. Eric Williams, George Padmore, John Jacob Thomas and Stokeley Carmichael.

The Black Jacobins, by C. L. R. James, came out in the late 1930s, during another of those turbulent periods in the Caribbean. Mr. James made a very close study of the slave society which is very important for an understanding of the West Indians and the era with which the book deals. The subject of the book is Toussaint L'Ouveture and the slave revolution in Haiti.

There had been large-scale slave revolts before in the New World, some led by men whose names have become well known, Makandal and Boukman, for example in the West Indies. In Brazil a black chief, Ganga Zumba, led a rebellion and established his own kingdom which he called 'The Palisade of Palm Trees' and which lasted for sixty-five years. Ganga Zumba repelled repeated military expeditions organised both by the Dutch and the Portugese. That War of the Palms occurred some forty years before the Maroon uprising in Jamaica.

Makandal in Haiti, was captured and burnt alive. There was a large-scale uprising in Suriname led by three men, Zan-Zan, Boston and Acaby. Even before that war was over there was another uprising in Haiti led by Boukman. Before that one was over there was another uprising in Trelawny in Jamaica, and another in Bahia in Brazil.

All those previous revolts had been crushed, but the one led by Toussaint L'Ouverture, the leader whom the Abbé Raynal had called for, that one the Europeans were unable to crush, and that was because slavery had done something to those Blacks which they could never forget.

In 1770, twenty-one years before the outbreak of the slave revolution in Haiti, the official census reported the population as follows: 30,000 Frenchmen, 24,000 Mulattos and 400,000 black slaves. Sainte Dominique (later re-named Haiti by the ex-slaves, the original Carib name), was then at the height of its prosperity. In 1791, all that prosperity was destroyed. We shall now examine why and how that happened.

We must remember that the slaves worked collectively on the plantations, even though they came from different African nations and from varying backgrounds. That is most important, for that kind of thing had never before happened in history, certainly not in Africa, neither in Europe as far as we know. That kind of existence did something to the Blacks is attested to by a French official, Roume, who had been in the island at the time. Roume had been fascinated by the manner in which the slaves had organised themselves: popular bodies, regiments, and so forth, and how those regiments soon became hardened by fighting. Five years after the Haitian revolution broke out, Roume wrote:

> *"Slogans and rallying cries were established between the chiefs of the sections and divisions and gave them points of contact from one extremity of the plains and towns of the north to the other. This guaranteed the leaders a means of calling out the labourers and sending back at will. These forms were extended to the districts in the West Province and were faithfully observed by the black labourers."*

The sociologist, psychologists and the people at the Universities working on their Masters and Doctorates may write what they like about Race and Intelligence, but Roume was on the spot, and what he tells us is what we must all recognise, those West Indian slaves were sufficiently clever to mobilise themselves and to impose self-discipline. Yet one hundred and fifty-four years later the people in Whitehall in England were saying that the West Indians would never be able to govern themselves. They have always misunderstood the West Indians, giving as their excuse for not handing over control of their affairs to the West Indians that they were 'training' those Blacks for Democracy, and 'preparing them for self-government.'

C.L.R. James proudly pointed out that in 1796 the people were illiterate; no one disputes that. Toussaint used to say that two-thirds of his people had made the Middle Passage and could not speak a European language. They knew a little French Creole, that was all. What was of primary importance, however, was that they worked together on the plantations, were masters of the technical skills required to run those plantations, and that made all the difference.

Since the slaves came from all classes of society, it would follow that amongst them would have been leaders and men of position back in Africa. Indeed, a Frenchman, Moreau de St. Mery, records that he had seen slaves who "recognise princes of their country prostrating themselves at their feet and rendering them that homage due even though they were all enslaved and undergoing the same treatment at the hands of the whites."

That would account for the discipline of the slaves, their ability to organise themselves and their readiness for war, so that their leaders were able to call them out and to send them back to work, or to their homes at will merely by the use of political slogans. Any population that can do that in 1796, asserts C. L. R. James, only five years away from slavery, a slavery which they had overthrown; any population that could do that was certainly fitted for absolute Parliamentary Democracy one hundred and fifty years later. Yet in 1950 the people in Whitehall were saying "No!" to the West Indians' demand for self-government.

After three hundred years of direct rule the British people had understood nothing about the West Indians. They misunderstood them in the Jamaica uprising of 1865; they misunderstood them in 1859, even though Joseph Chamberlain had supposedly recognised the economic problem in the West Indies, yet he did not permit the West Indians who were clamouring for it to do anything about it themselves. They misunderstood the West Indians in 1929; they misunderstood them in 1946. They misunderstood them again in Cuba in 1956.

to the slave revolt in Sainte Dominique. C.L.R. [...] after the defeat of the French, and of the British [...] ed that they would have succeeded where the French [...], Toussaint L'Ouverture came to a conception in 1801 [...] n could only be described in one word: genius.

Toussaint wrote a Constitution for Haiti and he did not submit it to the French for approval. He declared in that Constitution that Haiti would be governed by the ex-slaves. French officials, horrified, asked him what was the place of France in that Constitution. Toussaint replied "They will send Commissioners to speak with me."

It would appear that after the slaves were successful Toussaint had no intention of breaking off all links with France, even though the British had wished that to happen. Toussaint's plan was absolute independence on the one hand, but on the other, French capital, and French Commissioners to establish the relation between the two countries. He asked France to send a high official as a link between the two governments.

C. L. R. James says that all the evidence shows that Toussaint, working alone, had reached forward to that form of political relation which is known to-day as Dominion Status. Those West Indians had thought of it first, even though they did not know it as such; the word had not yet been invented, neither had been the idea. Toussaint's conception had anticipated the famous Durham Report by some forty years. Toussaint was far ahead of the politicians of his time. England only reached that point in Ottawa in 1932, when the English accepted the principle of complete independence of the old colonies, with a High Commissioner to speak to the local governments of Canada and Australia.

Fascinating that from the early days of their struggles the West Indians were laying down lines which could be followed without too much difficulty by their descendants, were it not for the obstacles which the people in Europe had put in their way. Toussaint knew and understood the Whites, that is why he introduced a literacy campaign and did not allow the Whites to get hold of the Blacks to educate them. Castro did the same in Cuba and succeeded in eradicating illiteracy in the island. In Britain the Colonial Office saw to it that when they handed over power it would be to those whom they had educated for that purpose. Hence the troubles which invariably followed independence in those former colonial territories.

Castro and Toussaint are both West Indians, the one White, the other Black, but the histories of their two countries are the same; they face the same obstacles. They are not exceptional men, they are just two West Indians. There have been men of Toussaint's persuasion since, with the same tremendous spirit, the same energy and political creativeness. Some of them we know and remember: Jean-Price Mars of Haiti, José Marti, Antonio Maceo and Fernando Ortiz of Cuba, William Gordon, Marcus Garvey of Jamaica, George Padmore and John Jacob Thomas, C. L. R. James, Captain Cipriani and Dr. Eric Williams of Trinidad, Albert Marryshow of Grenada, Sir Grantley Adams of Barbados, Aimé Césaire and Franz Fanon of Martinique, Leon Damas of French Guyana, Martin Carter of Guyana – The list is very long. That is the breed.

Toussaint, having ended slavery in Sainte Dominique (Haiti), then turned his sights towards Africa where he intended to sail in order to put an end to the slave trade there forever. The people in England got wind of this and there was genuine concern that Toussaint might invade Jamaica to end slavery there as well. Uprisings, therefore, were put down with the utmost brutalities in Jamaica. The British even imported bloodhounds to hunt down runaway slaves.

Pitt, having seen the writing on the wall, became a reluctant disciple of Adam Smith and, determined that the slaves must not liberate themselves, sought to find someone of impeccable character to do that for him in Parliament.

Pitt had his own political and economic reasons for wanting to end the slave trade – the rapid economic growth of Sainte Dominique. Pitt discovered that 50% of the slaves which were carried in the British ships were being sold to Sainte Dominique and the other French colonies. It was the British slave trade, then, that was increasing French colonial produce and putting Britain out of the market. Pitt saw that England was cutting its own throat. Worse, the French were getting their own slaves from Africa, and so were the Dutch and the Spaniards. In one year alone, 1784, the British had lost seven hundred thousand pounds sterling. That scandal had to be brought to an end. England would be able to beat the other nations, but, Pitt realised, with France that would require a full-scale war. If they got the world to stop the slave trade then France would be ruined economically and Sainte Dominique would be cut off completely.

Pitt asked Wilberforce to undertake the task. Wilberforce had a great reputation in the country and in Parliament and had absolutely no stain upon his character. It would sound well coming from him. In

1787 Pitt warned the reluctant Wilberforce that if he did not bring up the motion in the House, then somebody else would do it.

Pitt was in a desperate hurry. He knew that once he had ended the trade France had neither the capital nor the organisation such as England had in the form of the West India Committee to make good the deficiency at once, and he would thereby ruin Sainte Dominique.

There were people in England who seriously wanted abolition on humanitarian grounds. Those humanitarians never had a chance, as successive West Indian historians have discovered, including Dr. Eric Williams in his *Capitalism And Slavery*, and Miss Elsa Goveia in her writings. As Adam Smith had pointed out in his *Wealth Of Nations*, economic considerations were the decisive factors.

Not only in England. Thomas Carlyle informs us of the troubles which arose in France as a result of the revolution in Sainte Dominique when "not so much as sugar can be had," for "the plains of Cap Francais" is "one huge whirl of smoke and flames!" Carlyle reports that the ships were "rotting piecemeal in Harbour" and that "the shipping interest languish." He laughed, also, when the Quarteroon, Oge, one of the men who started the conflagration, was captured. Oge, "Repressed, doomed to die, he took black powder or seed grains in the hollow of his hand, this Oge; sprinkled a film of white ones on the top, and said to his Judges, 'Behold they are white;' then shook his hand, and said 'Where are the white ones?' Ou sont les Blancs?"

No doubt that was what Europe had feared, to be swallowed up by the Blacks. That treatment of the Whites by the Blacks, however, was not to be, for the time being, anyway. When that did come it was not because the Blacks wanted it, as we shall see later.

Europe had read the events in Sainte Dominique correctly. Of the man who was in the beginning at the head of those events, Toussaint L'Ouverture, C. L. R. James wrote:

> *"What spirit was it that moved him? Ideas do not fall from heaven. The great revolution had propelled him out of his humble joys and obscure destiny, and the trumpets of his heroic period rang over in his ears. In him, born a slave, and the leaders of slaves, the concrete realisation of liberty, equality and fraternity was the womb of ideas and the springs of power, which overflowed their narrow environment and embraced the whole of the world. But for*

the revolution, this extraordinary man and his band of gifted associates would have lived their lives as slaves, serving the commonplace creatures who owned them, standing barefoot and in rags to watch inflated little governors and mediocre officials from Europe pass by as many a talented African stands in Africa to-day."

That was written in 1938. The man thus described was a West Indian, ancestor of men such as George Padmore, Marcus Garvey, René Maran, Felix Eboué, Leon Damas, Stokeley Carmichael, Fernando Ortiz, Aimé Césaire, Derek Walcott, Sir Arthur Lewis, and a host of other distinguished West Indians who have made their mark upon the world stage, and contributed to Western Civilization.

Toussaint had been a stable-boy and he was forty-five when he led the revolution. He and his men defeated an army of 80,000 from Britain which, according to the military historian, Fortescue, was more than the British lost in the Peninsular War, a Spanish army of 50,000 Spaniards, and another army of 60,000 Frenchmen sent by Napoleon under the command of his brother-in-law, General Leclerc, with instructions to re-establish slavery in the West Indies. The West Indians drove them all off their land.

We must pause awhile to consider the amount of violence and bloodshed there has been throughout West Indian history. The society was founded on violence, was maintained by violence and, when the time came, it had to be destroyed by violence and bloodshed. That was what the West Indians had inherited from the Europeans in the West Indies. The West Indians had come to know nothing but violence and injustice from the very first to the last.

The result is that the West Indies, in the twentieth century, have produced some of the world's most notoriously bizarre regimes in the Western Hemisphere: Trujillo in the Dominican Republic, Duvalier in Haiti, Batista in Cuba, and a long line of others in Latin America. When those dictators came to power they built their regimes on what they had learned from the colonialists – violence. Sadism and brutal gangsterism. They brook no opposition, but destroyed all who dared opposed them. About that C. L. R. James says in his book *Party Politics in the West Indies:*

"It was as crude as that and they could do it because no tradition of democracy had been established in the country in

which they lived. The population had been trained to accept naked power and it was centuries of slavery and colonialism which had trained them."

The idea and practice of democracy had never been introduced to them nor had been practiced by the colonial powers when dealing with them. That tendency to naked power and naked brutality was the result of the West Indian experience. "You are ruled by an imperialist power" continues C.L. R. James:

" ... armed force decides. When you have slavery, you live with armed force every hour of the day. There is established not democracy, but subordination to power either actual or in reserve."

That has been the experience of both the upper and the lower classes in the West Indies. They have had no experience of any other life.

Toussaint had always trusted the Whites. Now in command and imagining that he could still trust them, he nevertheless kept an eye on them. One day he was invited to a banquet on board a visiting French warship, was tricked, arrested and packed off to France where he was made to languish in the cold of the Jura Mountains in Eastern France where he eventually died, with Napoleon not deigning to reply to any of his letters. When he died William Wordsworth, the English poet, wrote a moving poem about him:

TO TOUSSAINT L'OUVERTURE

Toussaint, the most unhappy man men!
Whether the whistling Rustic tend his plough
Within thy hearing, or thy head be now
Pillowed in some deep dungeon's earless den;-
O miserable Chieftain! Where and when
Wilt thou find patience! Yet die not; do thou
Wear rather in thy bonds a cheerful brow:
Though fallen thyself, never to rise again,
Live, and take comfort. Thou hast left behind
Powers that will work for thee; air, earth, and skies;
There's not a breathing of the common wind

THE OLD SYSTEM CRUMBLES

That will forget thee; thou hast great allies;
Thy friends are exaltations, agonies,
and love, and man's unconquerable mind.

Napoleon had won the first round; Toussaint was off the scene, but worse was to follow. Toussaint had taken Napoleon at his word that Sainte Dominique would remain free, but Napoleon had sent General Leclerc to work secretly in the background. Leclerc allowed the black and mulatto generals to remain at their posts until he thought the time ripe enough to strike. In his keeping were Napoleon's instructions:

"Follow your instructions exactly, and the moment you have rid yourself of Toussaint, Christophe and Dessalines, and the principal brigands, and the masses of the blacks have been disarmed, send over to the continent all the blacks and mulattos who have played a role in the civil troubles....Rid us of these gilded Africans, and we shall have nothing more to wish."

The moment Leclerc had succeeded in spiriting away Toussaint word reached Saint-Dominique that slavery had been restored in Guadeloupe and Martinique.

Saint-Dominique blew up overnight. The leader this time was Dessalines, the man to whom the Europeans liked to refer as the barbarian. Dessalines, indeed, hated everything white, but he was no barbarian until the Whites turned him into one. When that moment had been reached, according to one of his lieutenants, a man with the frightening name of Boisround Tonnerre, because he was so brutal, Dessalines is reported to have said:"To draw up the act of independence, we used the skin of a white man for parchment, his skull for inkwell, his blood for ink, and a bayonet for pen."

Under Dessalines the Blacks astonished the French soldiers with their skill and tenacity. They beat off repeated attacks and maintained a ceaseless harrying of the French posts, never allowing the French soldiers a moment's respite. What agonized the French soldiers even more was the guerrilla tactics to which the Blacks were resorting; that kind of warfare they had never known. The Blacks avoiding as much as possible any engagements with large French forces, disappearing into the mountains and leaving behind buildings and plantations in flames, and returning when the French soldiers, weary and having retreated to what they imagined were safe distances, only to be attacked once more from behind thickets and coverts by the Blacks, especially at nights, burning down more houses and killing white soldiers. The scorched earth tactics as far as the French were concerned was unconventional warfare.

Most of the mulattos had joined with their French fathers, adding to the complications of jealousy and rivalry between Blacks and Mulattos, Petits Blancs and Mulattos, and Grand Blancs.

In his book, *The Black Jacobins*, C. L. R. James examines the behaviour of the mulattos, and some of the Blacks who had become generals and administrators in the new government set up by France in Sainte Dominique. They would not join the revolution against the French attempt to re-impose slavery. The French had promised them a great deal and they had imagined that they would stand to gain nothing and lose too much when France became victorious, as it appeared to them that she would in the end.

Not all the mulattos. A few of them – Pétion, Boyer and Riviere-Herard – were later to take over after Dessalines and Christophe, and were to administer Haiti to the best of their ability.

Pétion was a moderate and, along with Christophe, they induced Dessalines to spare some of the Whites, in particular the Americans and some of the French who had sympathised with the slaves. They had done so in the hope that thereby they would retrieve their plantations after the war. In the case of the French that proved to have been a mistake on the part of the Haitian leaders, and we shall see why later, and the tragedy that followed.

The mulattos and those of the Blacks who had been promised much by the French, and who had taken the French at their word, were soon sadly deceived. The French singled out as their private property high-ranking officials and officers, men who had distinguished themselves on the battlefield, and had served with distinction in the new administration.

Christophe told the French General, Ramel, that if he thought slavery would be restored in Sainte Dominique, he would be mistaken. He would rather burn down the whole of Sainte Dominique before that happened. When the war broke out in earnest, a French historian who happened to have been on the spot, and who had been a member of Leclerc's expedition, described what happened:

THE OLD SYSTEM CRUMBLES

> *"But no one observed that in the new insurrection on San Domingo, as in all insurrections which attack constitutional authority, it was not the avowed chiefs who gave the signal for revolt, but the obscure creatures, for the most part personal enemies of the coloured generals."*

It was men like them, led by Dessalines, who finally led the masses to their freedom. Dessalines, the illiterate, who could not even write his own name, who had to have it traced for him in pencil for him to trace over in ink; he was the one who understood the Whites' good intentions that had been carved all over his back with the lashes of the whip.

Fifty years after the war of independence, a Frenchman who had been in General Leclerc's army, General Lamonier-Delafosse, wrote the following:

> *"But what men these blacks are! How they fight and how they die! One has to make war against them to know their reckless courage in braving danger when they can no longer have recourse to stratagem. I have seen a solid column, torn by grapeshot from four pieces of canon, advance without making a retrograde step. The more they fell, the greater seemed to be the courage of the rest. They advanced singing, for the Negro sings everywhere, makes songs about everything."*

The General continues later on:

> *"But for many a day that massed square which marched singing to its death, lighted by a magnificent sun, remained in my thoughts, and even to-day after more than forty years, this majestic and glorious spectacle still lives as vividly in my imagination as in the moments when I saw it."*

And from the man himself who had been sent by Napoleon with the expressed purpose of restoring slavery in the West Indies, the man who had commanded an army flushed with victories right across Europe to Russia, General Leclerc, the final words of defeat in his letter to Napoleon will also live, hauntingly, in Europe's mind: "We have in Europe a false idea of the country and the men against whom we fight."

One hundred and fifty years after emancipation in the West Indies, the ruling classes in Europe, led by those in England, were still trying to foster that same false idea about the West Indians.

The West Indians to-day are descended from the same stock and from the same kind of life which had made those ancestors of theirs what they were. Faced with the same difficulties the West Indians will respond in the same way. That response to injustice is inherent in them, descendants of those people who had made the Middle Passage, and had survived, and who had to learn all they could, and build a new life with what was gathered from the standards, the ideas, and the ideologies of the people and the new civilization in which they found themselves.

In fighting they had proved themselves the equal of Napoleon's army and those of Spain and Britain. We know what they did; we can deduce what their descendants are capable of doing. George Padmore, Franz Fanon, Marcus Garvey, Stokeley Carmichael, René Maran, Aimé Césaire and the others are their descendants. They and the present-day West Indians are of the same stock as those men and women who played such a great role in the history of their time. They are of the same stock as those Blacks in Jamaica, British and Dutch Guyana whom the British and the Dutch had had to fight full-scale wars, wars which those Europeans did not win.

To those Europeans it had been bad enough that the Blacks in Sainte Dominique had freed themselves and had declared Haiti an independent island republic. They felt even worse when the Blacks went further when they demonstrated proudly that 'black' was not simply an epithet, but a culture totem of considerable potency and authority. The white world was not only indignant, but frightened. Frightened because what the Haitians had announced was that they were not merely free of their former masters, white as well as mulatto, but that they were free of Europe itself. What the Haitians had also achieved was to have found an alternative to Judaic-Christian totalitarian democracy with its liberal pieties.

For years after the successful slave revolution in Haiti the Haitian ex-slaves haunted the imagination of the peoples of Europe, the United States of America and the Whites in the other West Indian islands. To have defeated the greatest powers at the time was bad enough. But the Haitians went further and said "No!" to the Judaic-Christian philosophy and theology and they replaced that theology with the worship of the Loas, that hierarchy of Voodoo gods and goddesses linked to the ancient pantheon of Dahomey, Guinea and the Congo.

Europe and the rest of the white world were not prepared to let Haiti get away with it. Their immediate reaction was to mount an economic campaign to ruin Haiti by instituting a blockade and a boycott of Haiti. Both Adam Smith and Professor Richard Pares in their respective works, *The Wealth of Nations* and *War And Trade In The West Indies*, have testified to the effectiveness of the economic blockade and the diplomatic isolation of Haiti from the rest of the world. The white world did not merely want to put those black upstarts, those ex-slaves, in their proper place, but, more than that, it was their counter-action to what they saw as black cultural subversion in the Western Hemisphere.

Because of the blockade, and the boycott, the island began to stagnate. No outsiders were permitted to have any dealings with Haiti. The country became inbred as a result; violence occurred. Tales of horrors, massacres and dictatorships were smuggled to the outside world.

West Indians have never changed their attitude to injustice as we shall see manifested in recent times.

During the Second World War (1939-1945), Sir Winston Churchill, at the time Prime Minister of Great Britain, had practically sold the West Indies to the United States of America for fifty destroyers, leasing the islands to the United States for ninety-nine years. Churchill returned later to sign the Atlantic Charter with President Franklin D. Roosevelt of the United States of America. That signing took place aboard a ship in Mid-Atlantic. While he was away signing the Charter, his deputy, Mr. Clement Atlee (Mr. Atlee was at the time Leader of the Labour Party in Britain), no doubt carried away by his Socialist ideals, called a Press Conference and outlined the details of that famous Charter by which subjugated peoples were going to be liberated after the war. Someone among the foreign journalists asked whether the Charter applied to black people as well to which Mr. Atlee answered in the affirmative. Sir Winston Churchill was informed about that upon his return to London and he put the record straight, when, in the House of Commons, in his rebuke of Mr. Clement Atlee, declared that Point Three of the Charter provided for "the right of peoples to choose the form of government under which they live and declared further that:

"We had in mind primarily the restoration of the sovereignty, self-government and national life of the states and nations of Europe now under the Nazi yoke....so that it is quite a separate problem from the progressive evolution of self-governing institutions in the regions which owe allegiance to the British Crown."

Churchill was not only rude to the Blacks; he also said some unkind things about Mahatma Ghandi and his Indian followers. To Churchill Ghandi was a "malignant subversive fanatic," and further declared that the Indian political party, the Indian Congress, did not represent the masses. Said Churchill:

"They merely represent those Indians who have acquired a veneer of Western civilization, and have read all those books which Europe is now beginning increasingly to discard."

The late Mr. George Padmore, a Trinidadian journalist who had been working in London at the time, understood perfectly what Sir Winston Churchill had said. When he received his call-up papers from the War Office, Padmore wrote back:

"If in this fifth year of war, the Mighty British Empire considers that its existence depends upon my active cooperation, then I am afraid that its chances of survival are slim, for I am prepared to face the maximum penalty for disregarding the summons and stand four square behind my political principles rather than be used as an instrument of imperial policy....I think it is a piece of bold effrontery to expect the victim of imperialism who is excluded from the lofty declarations of the Atlantic Charter, to contribute to the perpetuation of my own enslavement."

Padmore had no faith in the British Labour Party either, as he always said. In one of his pamphlets he reminded the Blacks in Britain, and in the colonies, that they can expect no hope under the rule of the British Labour Party:

"Remember, a British Socialist is a Briton first, and a socialist second. I don't believe there is such a thing as a 'British

> radical' – actually the words are contradictions. Even with them in power, the empire will never survive another storm, for the next war will be fought as an anti-racial and anti-imperialist war. There will be no more anti-fascist slogans to cover up the old racial racket of the British."

Once again we recognise the breed, the descendants of Toussaint, Dessalines, Maceo, Bogle, Gordon, and the others. They have not been crushed.

That is not all. Another West Indian, one who was not in England, but had heard and understood Churchill's words, was Dr. Eric Williams, at the time Chief Minister of Trinidad and Tobago.

The West Indians were looking for a site for the capital of the West Indies Federation, and Dr. Williams thought that the site that Sir Winston Churchill had given to the Americans for their base in the 'destroyer deal,' would be the ideal spot for the capital. In fact, a Committee which had been set up to investigate a possible site, had agreed on Chaguaramas where the Americans were. The West Indians asked for Chaguaramas, but the Americans said "No!" The British Government sided with the Americans.

Dr. Eric Williams stated that Chaguaramas was Trinidad property and that Churchill had no right to give away Trinidad property. "The only treaties we propose to acknowledge and honour," said Dr. Williams, "are those which we negotiate ourselves as equals. The 1941 Agreement is dead." Dr. Williams proposed to rid the West Indies "of the burdens unilaterally imposed by the 1941 Agreement."

The people of the West Indies agreed with him, because there were other American bases scattered amongst the islands.

At one of his meetings in Woodford Square, Port-of-Spain, Dr. Williams told the gathering that he would break Chaguaramas, or Chaguaramas would break him. As Chief Minister he could take certain actions, some of which he did and others he merely threatened to do. Since both Britain and America were adamant in their refusal to hand over Trinidad property, Dr. Williams addressed another meeting in Woodford Square and in a passionate and emotional speech he reminded his audience that for centuries the West Indies had been bases, the military football of warring imperialist powers, and that the time had come to finish with it. He entitled his speech that night 'From Slavery to Chaguaramas.'

Slavery, not very long ended in the West Indies, has never been forgotten, whether by Blacks, Whites or Mulattos. The precarious state of the economy, the insularity of the islands, as we have seen earlier, everything, in fact, the kind of relationship into which Europe had placed them for over three hundred years, have been due to the kind of system that had been imposed upon them.

Over this Chaguaramas issue both Europe and North America saw that the entire Caribbean was prepared to fight, and that rivers of blood would flow. Europe and North America took fright and gave in.

When we consider what the West Indians had been prepared to sacrifice – thousands of jobs on the U.S. bases – we can understand the measure of their feelings and their determination. It was a national upheaval and the West Indians were asserting their national identity. They were responding, as they have always done, to a grave situation.

The West Indians are a very politically conscious people; they understand Europe very well. It is Europe and North America that have to understand them. In the islands they had never ceased in their efforts to free themselves from slavery. When the Whites saw that they were prepared to take any steps to free themselves, they ended slavery so that they could make the Blacks believe that they were indebted to them. Some observers, however, were not to be deceived, and a Frenchman noted that:

> *"All the French Revolution has achieved is to legalise the Great Escape which has been going on since the 16th Century. The blacks didn't wait for you; they've proclaimed themselves free a countless number of times."*

That resolution by the Blacks in the West Indies was one of the most important steps in the making of the West Indian people. They were taking part in the destruction of European feudalism begun by the French Revolution, and liberty and equality, the slogans of the revolution, meant more to them than to any Frenchman. That was why, says C. L. R. James:

> *"That in the hour of danger Toussaint, uninstructed as he was, could find the language and accent of Diderot, Rousseau, and Raynal, of Mirabeau, Robespierre, and Danton. And in one respect he excelled them all. For even those masters of the*

spoken and written word, owing to the class complications of their society, too often had to pause, to hesitate, to qualify. Toussaint could defend the freedom of the Blacks without reservation, and this gave to his declaration a strength and a single-mindedness rare in the documents of the time. The French bourgeoisie could not understand it. Rivers of blood had to flow before they understood that elevated as was his tone Toussaint had written neither bombast nor rhetoric but the simple sober truth."

C. L. R. James was concluding his observations on the letter which Toussaint had written to the Directory in Paris after he had suspected Napoleon's intention to restore slavery which had been abolished after the success of the French Revolution. Toussaint had vowed "to bury ourselves under the ruins of a country revived by liberty rather than suffer the return of slavery ... We know how to face dangers to obtain liberty, we shall know how to brave death to maintain it."

Coming from a slave not six years out of slavery, bearing alone the burdens of government, and competing with the best minds in the Europe of the time, minds of men who had been formed in the tradition of ethics, philosophy and the history of Western civilization, we cannot but admire and admit, unhesitatingly, that that West Indian was in the forefront of the great historical movement of his time.

Those are the things which must be taught in the schools not only in the West Indies, but in Europe and the United States of America as well, for it will help people to understand what went into making the West Indians the kind of people that they are.

The Europeans never introduced democracy in the Caribbean. They introduced slavery and they followed the abolition of slavery with the Crown Colony Government, or Democracy limited only to the white planters. They created a society destitute of learned leisure, of liberalism, of literacy and scientific intercourse. Indeed what they created, in short, was a philistine society. The West Indians have, as a consequence, inherited an awful historical past. That is the heritage that they have had to fight, and of which they still bear the scars.

" ... J'arriverais lisse et jeune dans
ce pays mien et je dirais à ce pays dont le limon
entre dans la composition de ma chair : 'J'ai
longtemps erré et je reviens vers la hideur désertée
de vos plaies.'
Je vendrais à ce pays mien et je lui dirais :
'Embrassez-moi sans crainte...Et si je ne sais que
parler, c'est pour vous que je parlerai.'

Et je lui dirais encore :

'Ma bouche sera la bouche des malheurs qui
n'ont point de bouche, ma voix, la liberté de celles
qui s'affaissent au cachot du désespoir.'

(" ... I should arrive lithe and young in this country of mine
and I should say to this land
whose mud is flesh of my flesh 'I wandered for a long time and I am returning to the deserted
foulness of your wounds."

I should come back to this land of mine and
Say to it: 'Embrace me without fear ... If all
I can do is speak, at least I shall speak for you.'

And I should say further:

'My tongue shall serve those miseries which
have no tongue, my voice the liberty of those who
founder in the dungeons of despair.')

CHAPTER 3
The Literature of Revolt

WE SHALL NOW CONSIDER MORE EVIDENCE OF WHAT the West Indians have done, and what they are capable of doing.

The West Indies are very much part of the Western World. Situated as the islands are between the two most industrial continents of the world, North America and Western Europe, they are subjected constantly to all the latest fads and fancies from those two giants.

We know the kind of relationship that had been established between Europe and the West Indies. That relationship is part of the West Indian heritage, and it is that heritage which the West Indians will carry into the future.

From Columbus down to the present Europe has always been very fond of defining other peoples, and the West Indians have suffered, and are still suffering their share of that inclination of the Europeans. First they were heathens and barbarians who were taken from Africa to the West Indies. Then later they were West Indians. To-day they are people of the "Third World."

It is that game that Europe is always playing, defining and re-defining other peoples and which creates confusion, putting those peoples into categories to suit Europe itself. It all has to do with what the Barbadian writer, George Lamming, refers to as the Europeans' certain way of looking at and seeing other peoples.

The West Indians understood very well what had been done to them, but in order to throw off that heritage that had been left behind they had to set about defining themselves, forcing Europe to alter its particular way of looking at and seeing them. The expression of that new outlook, that Identity, is to be found in the literature created by the West Indians.

We look, then, at that literature. The modern West Indian writer was not concerned with following any tradition because he did not have any. What he did have, however, was irrepressible confidence, unlimited energy and, above all, impatience.

The West Indian writer is using a language that is not his own; a language which, whether he writes in English, French, Spanish or Dutch, is a language that had been fashioned over the centuries by the people of Europe and therefore bore all the marks of their history, traditions and experiences. The West Indian slaves learned those languages, and learned them well; they had to in order to survive. From their very first introduction to Western Christian civilization they had to learn the language of their master, since no two slaves from the same tribe were ever put to work together, as Richard Ligon had informed us in his book *A True And Exact History of the Island of Barbados*. The language that they learned, whether it was English, French or Dutch, was not their own, so that for the West Indian writer the language did not express the experiences of his people from the relative freedom and communal life of his African past, through the Middle Passage into slavery, into emancipation and the hazards and dilemmas of the modern age.

The West Indian writer, therefore, had to do something with that acquired language in order to make that language his own, to speak for him and for his people. He had to manipulate that language, to do violence to it where necessary; to break it up and mould it to express the West Indian's own unique feeling, his own unique experiences. In short, to express the West Indian consciousness.

Now, what is meant by that West Indian consciousness? Or a people's consciousness, for that matter?

It means the sum total of a people's thoughts and feelings, and the response to those experiences which are common to all human beings: love, birth, marriage, pain and death. That response is conditioned by a people's history, and the history of the West Indies is a history of disruption, chaos, violence and injustice; the disruption and chaos of slavery and the slave trade, and the violence and injustice necessary to maintain the system and the slave society. After four hundred years of such a system, that kind of existence and experience has left its mark. We see it to-day in the West Indian's attitude to a number of things – marriage and concubinage, diet, religion, authority, for example.

We shall look at some of the other effects of slavery in a later chapter which will deal with the pattern of culture which finally emerged in the Caribbean.

Concerning marriage and concubinage, for instance, we must remember that the slaves were not permitted to marry in the British and Dutch West Indies. In the French and Spanish islands they were permitted to marry, but with the permission of their masters. The Portuguese encouraged mixed marriages. In the British and Dutch West Indies, as Father Labat had observed, the slaves were encouraged to reproduce as many children as possible, and the male slaves to have as many wives as they liked. There was also the introduction of the slave stud farm and the indignities to which the black slave women were subjected by both black and white males. The mulatto children, because of their lighter complexion, fetched a higher price on the market, and were, as a general rule, made house slaves when they were not freed. That practice was later to introduce tremendous distress in the West Indies – the favoured position of the people of colour – les gens de couleur – in West Indian society. Such things have left their mark on the West Indian consciousness.

The Europeans in the West Indies never considered the islands as their home. That was to affect the society and the culture which eventually emerged. Again, in that slave society, where black slaves and white masters had to live in such close proximity to each other because of the size of the islands, a kind of relationship was established which had never existed in the world before. Those things also left their mark – the fact that the West Indian Blacks have always taken the white presence for granted.

Then came emancipation and the introduction of the East: India and China, Java and Indonesia. To-day in the Caribbean there is a very unique society, the product of a very unique history—an amalgam of peoples and cultures, often described as a melting pot, so to speak, which has resulted in the creation of a unique culture—Creole culture, which has resulted, also, in the West Indian's cosmopolitanism; he is at home anywhere any everywhere. That becomes natural to him because he grew up in that atmosphere of races and peoples of varying complexions, beliefs and practices. He is, in short, the living integrationist. Commenting on that cosmopolitanism, the Barbadian writer, George Lamming writes:

> *"What most of the world regard to-day as the possibility of racial harmony has always been the background of the West Indian prospect. Racial integration will be an achievement of the American school. In the West Indies it is the background against which learning has taken place. We in the West Indies can meet the twentieth century without fear; for we begin with colossal advantages."*

Black, white, brown, whatever the race – they're all West Indians and they have all come to think like that. In the West Indies they all face the same problems and the same dilemmas. Indeed, some of the harshest critics of European and North American racial, political and economic policies have been white West Indians, whether they come from Cuba, Haiti, Puerto Rico, Jamaica or Trinidad and Tobago.

Having said that we can now state that Literature, being one of the most important aspects in the development of a people's culture, is thus an indication that certain creative people in the society have taken the initiative in reconstructing their conception of their society, of themselves and of the world about them, and have taken upon themselves the task of creating order out of chaos. In the West Indies that chaos was slavery and indentured labour and what followed – Colonialism.

The mission of the man of letters, therefore, in early Caribbean writing, was, first abolition of slavery. Those anti-slavery novels, poems and plays came first from the white Cubans. That literature is important because it has left us with a record of an aspect of Caribbean society which the Europeans to-day would be only too happy to hide, or to gloss over.

Slavery was finally abolished in the Caribbean in 1886, but as a subject of literature it continues to occupy many poets to this day. Every major and minor poet in the Caribbean at one time or another has dealt with the subject. Every occasion, every incident, every experience, racial or otherwise, brings the subject to mind immediately. Thus the poet. Jean Brierre of Haiti, looking at the Negroes in Harlem, recalls the common sufferings of the past, and says:

"Together we knew the horror of the slave ships, and often like me you feel the cramps awaking after the murderous centuries and you feel the wounds bleed in your flesh."

From Cuba another poet recalls the sufferings and humiliations of slavery, and he reminds his listeners that:

"The lash of the overseer punished our sides with fear so we would walk with the docility of bridled ponies along with the oxen ... "

The most famous of Cuba's poets, the mulatto, Nicolas Guillen, evokes the horrors of slavery with much bitterness and in a long poem he asks the Europeans what have they done with his name, the name of his African ancestors? Slavery had robbed the Blacks of everything – their homeland, their language, their names, their religion, and Guillen says "We must learn to remember, what the clouds cannot forget" ("Hay que aprender a recordar lo que las nubes no pueden olvidar")

In the years immediately following the first world war (1914-1918), there took root amongst the writers in Cuba and the rest of the Caribbean, a concern for the negro in which the writers made the Negro their central preoccupation, probing deep into the life of the Negro element in the society as a whole. That movement which came to be known as Afro-Cubanism, started in Cuba where the Negro has always been in the minority. That movement coincided with the advent in Europe of a very critical reaction to the whole of Western culture. That re-examination of Western culture in Europe was responsible for the world-wide recognition of the Afro-Cuban movement. The black American writer, Langston Hughes, has recorded the effect that that re-examination of Western culture had on the New Negro Renaissance in North America – the Harlem Renaissance.

The man, however, who really exploded the myth of Western European cultural superiority, and exposed the failure of Western Christian civilization, was the German philosopher, Oswald Spengler who had published a book in 1917, entitled *The Decline Of The West*. People in Europe were disillusioned by the 1914–1918 war. That disillusion was understandable, for Europe, having for centuries boasted of her achievements in science, philosophy and other theories of Western progress, had suddenly and brutally discredited herself by one of the most atrocious wars that humanity had ever experienced.

Two eminent critics, Professor Eric Heller in *The Disinherited Mind* and Lionel Trilling in *The Middle Of The Journey*, have both stated why they dislike Spengler's *The Decline Of The West*. Lionel Trilling says in *The Middle Of The Journey*, that he dislikes the book "because it has so hideous a possibility of being true," and likens Spengler to the horribly callous physician who told us of our unknown and unsuspected disease.

Professor Heller himself notes that Spengler's "ill-tempered prophecies have unfortunately come true," and observes further that the history of the West since 1917 "looks like the work of children clumsily filling in with lurid colours a design drawn in outline by Oswald Spengler."

Indeed, the spiritual exhaustion of the age has been the dominant theme of North America's and Europe's most discussed writers: D.H. Lawrence, Franz Kafka, T. S. Eliot, Arthur Koestler, William Burroughs, Henry Miller, and the films coming out of Hollywood. Even those writers like Aldous Huxley and George Orwell, who indulge in prophetic visions of the future, merely elaborate the themes from 'The Decline Of The West.'

Spengler's book had a profound influence on writers and artists in the Caribbean when the book first appeared. With the appearance of Spengler's book the West Indian writers of the time were unable any longer to accept Europe's high-sounding phrases and theories of progress, civilization, ethics and morality, freedom, equality, liberty and the brotherhood of man. Claude McKay of Jamaica, for example, writing in the first quarter of the last century, in several of his poems condemns the white world for its hypocrisy. In one of his poems in the collection *Selected Poems* with an introduction by John Dewey, the poem entitled *To The White Friends*, McKay says that he could just as well be as evil as they are, and for their dastardly deeds he could out-match theirs:

> *But the Almighty from the darkness drew*
> *My soul and said: Even thou shall be a light*
> *Awhile to burn on the benighted earth,*
> *Thy dusky face I set among the white*
> *For thee to prove thyself of higher worth;*
> *Before the world is swallowed up in night*
> *To show thy little lamp: go forth, go forth!"*

Another West Indian poet, this time from the French Antilles, put into words what that discovery had done to him, and boasts:

> "And I overcome
> By a pompous coup d'état,
> All the cloudy disciplines of my childhood
> Hatched in the new soil of my consciousness."

That West Indian consciousness about which we heard earlier.

It was during that period of intense crisis that the literary fashion for the Negro was born, and African and Neo-African art became the fashion of the times in Europe. Josephine Baker, the black American dancer, and Louis Armstrong, the Jazz musician, became the vogue in Europe, lionized and feted by Royalty and High Society alike.

It was also during that period of intense spiritual crisis, with the death of Western culture, and with Europe exhausted and having worked out its artistic possibilities, that artists and intellectuals in Europe turned to Africa for inspiration and a chance to live again. In the 1920s African sculpture and African painting became the vogue. Leo Frobenius, a German anthropologist, published his book, *The Black Decameron*, in which he drew attention to the value and importance of African art. Picasso and the cubists were overwhelmingly influenced by African art. Andre Breton 'discovered' Aimé Césaire's 'Cahier D'un Retour Au Pays Natal' (Journal Of A Return To My Native Land), one of the most incisive criticisms of Western Christian civilization. In the whole of Western European art and literature, we find a critical reaction to Western culture.

To some of the European writers and artists it was merely a fashion, to some others it was their way of showing dissatisfaction with the established values. With the Caribbean writers and artists it had a greater and more profound significance. They were writing from within and were thus able to make known to the world the special sensibility of the Negro people. They exalted in every aspect of Negro life, stressing his sensuality, his emotionalism, his realism, his own rhythmic use of language, his music and his dances. Above all, what they were engaged in was in setting those up as a corrective to the over-civilization of the white world with all its attendant physical, moral and spiritual maladies.

That reaction against Western values took many forms in West Indian writing. There were the writers who, Like Jacques Roumain of Haiti, in that rejection, looked to Africa for their spiritual renaissance. Roumain takes the slow road to Guinea. On the other hand there were those West Indian writers who looked at West Indian life and said, very well, this is ours; this is us, our heritage. Let us not be ashamed of it. Let us sing about it. Let us dance to it. Let us paint it. If the Whites like it, that's fine. If they do not like it, that's fine, too. So we hear Aimé Césaire saying to the Whites "Take me as I am. I won't accommodate myself to suit you!" And Philippe Thoby Marcelin "Swearing an eternal scorn for the refinements of Europe" and joyfully singing "in a new voice the de profundis of your rotting civilization."

Some of the writers, like Leon Damas of French Guyana, even resented the wearing of European clothes, saying how ridiculous he feels in them, while Georges Desportes of Haiti proclaims his pride in being a Negro, and " The glory of being black."

Those West Indian writers were repelling, indeed rejecting, all the negative, debilitating influences of Western European culture. Even the nature of the school curriculum was attacked, considering it alien to them. The poet, Guy Tirolien of Guadeloupe, does not want the children to become copies of the Whites who can neither dance , nor walk barefoot; who have lost the power and charm of naturalness; who no longer sense the marvellous in Nature, nor can relate stories and folk tales by the light of the moon. Folk tales about Compère Lapin 'et bien d'autre choses qui ne sont pas dans leurs livres.' That is most beautifully expressed in his poem *Prière D'un Petit Enfant Nègre* (Prayer of a Little Negro Boy). The little boy keeps repeating that he does not want to go to their school. Instead, he says:

> '*Je préfère*
> *vers l'heure ou la lune amoureuse*
> *parle bas à l'oreille*
> *des cocotiers penches*
> *écoutez ce qui dit*
> *dans la nuit*
> *la voix cassée d'un vieux qui raconte en fumant*
> *les histoires de Zamba*
> *et de Compère Lapin*
> *et bien d'autres choses encore*
> *qui ne sont pas dans leurs livres.*'

Again, because of the role the established churches had played in the maintenance of the slave society, they have been subjected to some bitter attacks from the poets. Writing in 1939, Jacques Roumain says that "In the cellars of the monasteries the priest counts the interest on the thirty pieces of silver" and in another poem he rejects Christianity outright, and says:

> "...*we don't give a damn*
> *for a God who,*

> *if he is the father,*
> *well, we, the dirty niggers*
> *it is obvious that we must be his bastard sons*
> *and it won't help yelling*
> *Jesus Mary Joseph*
> *Like an old bladder spilling over with lies."*

From almost every quarter the attacks were violently abusive. When they were not so, some of the poets used sarcasm, as was the case with Paul Niger from Guadeloupe.

Most of those writers turned instinctively to Africa, the cultural and spiritual home of the black people for their sustenance and guidance. Africa has never been forgotten in the West Indies, for it is the memory of Africa which had helped the Blacks to survive in the West Indies. As it was necessary for them to remember Africa, so, too, they could never forget why they had been torn from their ancestral homeland. So the deep persistent memory of slavery remains. The wounds still ache, red and inflamed. That heritage which he carries with him wherever he goes, his experiences during his wanderings about the world, his exile—all those things bring back memories of that enslavement, and the rivers of blood which flowed from the whip-lashed wounds. His history is one of suffering, violence and injustice. His memory is soaked in blood. So we hear Aimé Césaire bemoaning "How much blood in my memory, in my memory are lagoons ... " And Guy Tirolien sighing dolefully:

> *"I know only the history inscribed in my flesh*
> *by the fire of whips*
> *the burn of packing sticks*
> *of red hot irons*
> *and of rape."*

What a heritage for a people!

For another poet, Jorge Artel, when he hears the drums being played, he remembers Africa. It is the memory of Africa, and his confidence in the strength of Africa that has helped the West Indian to survive. The confidence in himself, also, because of the African blood that has taken root in the Caribbean, such being the resilience of that blood. In a poem entitled *Afrique* Guy Tirolien says:

> "*Tes surgeons refleurissent, Afrique,
> dans la chair labourée de mon peuple,
> car tu germais en moi depuis la nuit des temps*"

and continues later in the poem:

> "*Branche vivre arrachée à l'arbre motilé,
> j'ai repoussée plus dur sur le sol étranger
> car ma race est vivace et beaucoup plus tenace
> que l'acacia qui pousse a Saint Dominique.*"

> (*Your shoots flower again, Africa,
> in the ripped flesh of my people
> for your seed has lain in me since the night of all time.*)

> *Live branch torn from a mutilated tree
> I have grown again even stronger in alien soil
> For my race is perennial and much more tenacious
> Than the tough acacia that grows in Saint-Dominique*)

The West Indian poet also rejected the European concept of love and beauty. He mocked the unnaturalness and coldness of the white female, and praised the beauty and sensuality of the black and mulatto woman. When the white writer portrayed the black woman she was never a figure to inspire admiration or love, but only of lust. Occasionally, as in Baudelaire's *A Une Dame Creole* the white poet paid tribute to her beauty and charm, but that is rare. Le Conte de Lisle (a white West Indian, along with Baudelaire was part of the Romantic Movement in France).

When the time came to write about the black West Indian woman, the West Indian poet, Philippe Thoby Marcellin, joined with his other fellow West Indian poets , and says in his poem *Petite Noire* "I shall sing of you, little black girl, it is your hour now ... "

Eight years after Pierre Faubert had published his poem, *The Negress*, praising her black colour, Oswald Durand, in 1884, published a poem in the French Creole language entitled *Choucoune*, the name of the Haitian peasant girl from the hills, one of the most beautiful poems about the black woman. That poem has been set to music, and in English has been given the title *Yellow Bird*.

In praising the black woman the West Indian poet also revealed contempt for the white woman which is shown most blatantly in a poem by French Guyana's Leon Damas, in which he refers to her as "those pale vendors of love who come and go along the boulevards of my boredom." He calls, instead, for his black women, and says in the poem entitled *Limbé*:

> "Give me back my black dolls
> so that I may play again with them
> the naïve games of my instincts,
> Stay in the shadow of its laws.
> Recover my courage, my daring,
> Feel myself again, my new self
> which I was yesterday,
> Yesterday, without complexity,
> Yesterday, at the time of the uprooting."

In yet another of his more nostalgic poems entitled *Black Beauty*, Guy Tirolien, looking at some black girls dancing in the village, remembers Africa and, in lines most lyrical, says how they remind him of his dark and naked sisters in Guinea, and that they arouse in him the heavy black twilight of sensuous excitement. ("font lever en moi ce soir des *crépuscules* negres lourds d'un sensual èmoi").

The white woman, then, having been driven from the boulevards of his memory after his sojourn in Europe, the poet could now reaffirm the beauty, gracefulness, seductiveness and spontaneity, the warmth and naturalness of the black woman. He sang of her black and brown body undulating and unwinding itself in the slow concentric movements of the dance, of the free movements of her hips when she walked, or when she made love. To him she represents sensuality and fertility.

Lionel Attuly of Martinique, says to her that he has found again his place in the hollow of her shoulders, on her breast a real breast (J'ai retrouvé ma place aux cruex de ton épaule, Sur ton sein un vrai scin…)

Those poems were written between 1800 and 1939. That may surprise many people, especially when they read, or hear of what is being written to-day by poets who themselves are using the same language of vituperation and slander, rejection and revolt, abuse and sarcasm when looking at Western Christian civilization. Those feelings expressed the West Indian poet's reaction to that civilization, and were produced as a corrective to the over-mechanized European way of life, and of the false values which Europe had propagated for so long, values of morality and such like.

Not only the West Indian poets, but the African as well, were critical of Western civilization. Leopold Sedar Senghor from Senegal, for example, on a visit to New York can only see "blue metallic eyes" and "frosty" smiles, "No children's laughter blossoms," "No tender words for mouths are lipless. Hard cash buys artificial hearts." And New York was where "dark waters bear away hygienic loves, like the bodies of children on a river in flood" (... les eaux obscures des amours hygieniques, tells des fleuves en crue des cadaves d'enfants.)

The West Indian had chosen no longer to look to Europe for guidance, at least in so far as matters of morality and spiritual affairs were concerned. In a final burst of rejection, Aimé Césaire lists all the things that Europe is supposed to represent and which she shows that she really cares nothing about both by her actions and by the millions of her children she sacrificed in wars every twenty-five years. Césaire then tells us what Europe really means to him "Europe, Pompous name for excrement."

Such harsh criticism would have offended many people, but perhaps what Césaire wanted was for us to remember West Indian history, and what was being said about, and what was being done to the Blacks during the four hundred years of slavery in the Caribbean and the Western Hemisphere. The West Indian writers felt that they had to do that; they had to use vituperation and slander on occasions, because they needed first to destroy that edifice upon which white civilization had based its racial arrogance.

In 1947 the French philosopher and novelist, Jean-Paul Sartre was invited to write an introduction to an anthology of Negro writing in which the majority of the contributors were West Indians. Sartre entitled his introduction *Orphée Noir*, Black Orpheus, and it was one of the very first attempts at examination and interpretation ever written about the writings of black poets. Sartre begins his introduction with the questions:

> *"Just what were you hoping when you removed the gags from all these black mouths? That they were going to sing your praises? And when the heads that our fathers had brought down to the earth rose up, did you expect to read adoration in their eyes? Here are men, standing, looking at us, and I wish that you*

THE LITERATURE OF REVOLT

might feel as I do the thrill of being seen. For 3,000 years the white man has enjoyed the privilege of looking without being seen; he did nothing but look; the light of his eyes drew forth all things from their native shadow, the whiteness of his skin, condensed light, was another way of looking. The white man, white because he was man, white as day, white as truth, white as virtue, lit up all creation like a torch, revealing the essence, secret and white, of its creatures. To-day these black men are returning our looks, staring down at us; they are, in their turn, black torches lighting the world and our white heads are not more than Chinese lanterns buffeted by the wind."

It was now time for the black man to define himself, and the white man would have now to accept his definition. Having thus made the white world feel ill at ease by attacking and undermining their security, the West Indian writers made the white world listen to them, and to what they had to offer. What they had to offer was that sense of life that Europe had lost long ago. Europe, having dehumanized her very own people, the black writers were saying now to Europe the gun powder, the bacteria for warfare, the concentration camps, the gas chambers, were not the limits of man's progress.

The poem which makes that abundantly clear is Aimé Césaire's *Cahier D'Un Retour Au Pays Natal*.

Poet, playwright, essayist and politician, Césaire is one of the world's foremost black intellectuals. For several years he represented his country, Martinique, in the National Assembly in Paris and he had been Mayor of his island's capital city, Fort-de-France for an equal number of years. André Breton, the high priest of Surrealism, has described with something of awe, his first meeting with Aimé Cesairé, and André Malraux, coming several years later, has described his meeting with that remarkable man in Martinique, in his autobiography, *Anti-Memoires*.

The former colonies of France have become assimilated and are now Overseas Departments. Now that France has joined the European Union, Martinique French Guyana and Guadeloupe in the Caribbean are now part of Europe, Europe in the Caribbean. Their currency is now the Euro. There had been several black French nationals who had been Ministers in various French Governments. One of them was the late Leopold Sedar Senghor of Senegal. Before and during President De Gaule's term in office, the man who was

President of the Upper House in Paris, the equivalent of the House of Lords in the United Kingdom, was a black West Indian, Gaston Monnerville. Another black West Indian, Felix Eboué, had been Governor-General of what was then French West Africa.

Martinique, Aimé Césaire's birthplace, is also the home of René Maran, Franz Fanon, Eduoard Glissant, Patrick Chamoiseau, Joseph Zobel, and several others. René Maran was one of the first West Indian novelists to take up his pen in defence of the Africans. Like Fanon after him he had been a civil servant in Africa, but he lost his appointment, but gained world-wide fame in the process when in 1921, his first novel, *Batouala*, was published attacking French colonialism in Africa. The novel won the Prix Goncourt for Maran.

When Aimé Césaire went to school in Martinique he studied the French language, French Literature, French Philosophy, Greek and Latin. At High School the subjects were the same. At University in Paris he, again, read the same subjects. Throughout his academic life, therefore, Césaire had steeped himself in European thought and civilization. When he came to write, however, he produced, in his famous poem, *Cahier D'Un Retour Au Pays Natal,* one of the most incisive and devastating attacks upon Western Christian civilization. He was able to do that because he had studied and come to know that civilization only too well. That is why he had been able to take that civilization to pieces. In a short book entitled *Discourse On Colonialism* Césaire stated that that civilization was morally and spiritually indefensible.

It was in that long poem '*Cahier* ... ' that Césaire first propounded the concept of Negritude. Much has been written about Negritude and it has been the subject of much debate and controversy. The three books which were written by non-West Indians and which impressed me are *De La Negritude Dans La Litterature Negro-Africain* by Thomas Melone of the Cameroons, West Africa , *Les écrivains noirs de langue francais: Naissance d'une litterature* by Madame Lilyn Kestleloot from Belgium and *Negritude Et Humanisme* by the late Leopold Sedar Senghor, one-time President of Senegal in West Africa.

Leopold Senghor has defined it, first saying that "It is time to define this word which so lends itself to polemical and to contradictory interpretations. Quite simply, Negritude is the sum total of the values of the civilization of the African world. It is not racialism, it is culture. It is the embracing and domination of the cosmos by the process of coming to terms with it."

Negritude, then, is the awareness, the defence and development of African cultural values.

In defining their values the Europeans found it necessary, first, to degrade those of the black people and to make them despise their own. Both Mannoni in his *Prospero and Caliban – The Psychology of Colonization*, and Albert Memmi in his *The Colonizer and the Colonized*. have gone into great detail about how Europe had set about doing that, and the response of the colonized which often resulted in that feeling of 'dependence' and 'inferiority.'

As far back as the German philosopher, Hegel, in his *Philosophy of History*, he had found it necessary to entertain a very discreditable and highly misconceived idea of Africa and of black people in general. Hegel wrote:

> *"Africa proper, as far as History goes back, has remained—for all purposes of connection with the rest of the world—shut up; it is the Gold-land compressed within itself—the land of childhood, which lying beyond the day of self-conscious history, is enveloped in the dark mantle of night."*

Hegel then goes on to say that:

> *"The peculiar African character is difficult to comprehend, for the very reason that in reference to it, we must quite give up the principle which naturally accompanies all our ideas—the category of Universality."*

Hegel does not stop there, but continues to make this statement:

> *"The Negro, as already observed, exhibits the natural man in his completely wild and untamed state. We must lay aside all thoughts of reverence and morality – all that we call feeling – if we would rightly comprehend him: there is nothing harmonious to be found in this type of character."*

Hegel then goes on to discredit African religions and quotes the Greek historian, Heredotus, who called the Africans sorcerers. Hegel agrees with the Greek and adds that "in sorcery we have not the idea of a God, of a moral faith."

Leopold Senghor has dealt at length with Hegel on those points. So have a number of African cultural anthropologists, some theologians from France and Britain. So have Aimé Cesairé and George lamming, who expressed surprise, and annoyance that so profound a thinker as the American Negro, James Baldwin, had cowered before Hegel's onslaught. In his slim volume of essays, *Notes Of A Native Son*, James Baldwin, in reflection on his own development as a person and a writer, says that he was forced to recognize that he was a bastard of the West, and goes on:

> " ... when I followed the line of my past I did not find myself in Europe but in Africa. And this meant that in some subtle way, in a really profound way I brought to Shakespeare, Bach, Rembrandt, to the stones of Paris, to the Cathedral at Chartres, and to the Empire State Building, a special attitude. These were really not my creations; they did not contain my history; I might search in them in vain for ever for any reflection of myself; I was an interloper. At the same time I had no other heritage which I could possibly hope to use - I had certainly been unfitted for the jungle or the tribe. I would have to appropriate these white centuries. I would have to make them mine - I would have to accept my special attitude, my special place in this scheme - otherwise I would have no place in any scheme."

In the following sentence Baldwin confesses to something he has had to hide from himself, that all black Americans have had to hide from themselves, "that I hated and feared white people." That fear and hatred of white people and, by extension, the world, Baldwin admits to giving them "an altogether murderous power over me ... "

That is precisely what has not happened to the black West Indian in the West Indies. The West Indian has never felt that overwhelming fear of the white people, for he has always taken the white presence for granted; there has never been that overwhelming superiority of white people in the West Indies.

Hence the importance of Negritude, the weapon of defence and attack. Above all, of inspiration. It was the awareness of a particular people, the black people, of their situation in the world, and the expression of that situation by means of a concrete image. Negritude is made up of human warmth. It is democracy quickened by the sense of communion and brotherhood between men.

It is a sense of rhythm and image; a sense of symbol and beauty expressed in works of art which are, insists Senghor, a people's authentic expression of itself. It strives for pan-human socialization. It is, above all, the black people's supreme contribution to the building of the Civilization of the Universal.

There have been certain books which have greatly influenced men's minds: the *Bible*, Rousseau's *Du Contract Social*, Paine's *The Rights Of Man*, Pericles on *Democracy*,' Karl Marx's *Das Capital*. From the Caribbean have come three : *The Black Jacobins* by C. L. R. James, Franz Fanon's T*he Wretched of the Earth*,' Aimé Césaire's *Cahier D'Un Retour Au Pays Natal*.

A whole generation of black writers in Africa, Brazil, the Caribbean and North America were influenced by Césaire's book. German intellectuals have been fascinated by the book, and one of them, Professor Janheinz Jahn (*Muntu* and *A History of Neo-African Literature*), from Brussels. Madame Lilyan Kesteloot's *Les Ecrivains Noirs du Langue Francaise : Naissaince d'une Litterature*. From the University of Zagreb in Jugoslavia has also come a very lucid exposition upon the meaning and purpose of the writer, Aimé Cesairé, from one of the Professors, Peter Guberina. Professor Guberina likens Césaire's '*Cahier ...* ' to Dante's *Inferno*. And says that:

> "*La vérité essentielle que nous dégageons du poème de Césaire, 'Cahier d'un Retour au Pays Natal,' se ramène à ceci: c'est l'enfer que surgit le paradis. Il faut descendre en enfer pour se purifier.*"

But the poem, continues the Professor, "devient ainsi un poème en faveur de la liberté de l'homme en général."

What, then, has Césaire attempted to do in that poem? What is he saying?

Césaire is suggesting that through his suffering the black man has learned something of immense importance. From the point of view of Europe, Negro life is negative. But, Césaire maintains, in that very negativeness the Negro possesses something of immense value, something which Europe has lost. Having discovered his own values the Negro now feels a certain pride and joy in his discovery that, after all, there is still work to be done ... ("car il n'est point vrai que l'ouevre de l'homme est finie ... "). Indeed, that the real work of man is only now beginning (que l'ouvre de l'homme viente seulement de commencer) and that the negro must now step boldly forward to make his contribution. For the moment, however, it will be through his art and his literature, through his way of life, his music and his dances that he must strive to rejuvenate the world. He is the leaven which the white flour needs, to quote Senghor. For, says Senghor:

> *"...who else would teach rhythm to a world*
> *that has died of machines and cannons?*
> *For who else would ejaculate the cry of joy*
> *that arouses the dead and the wise in a new dawn?*
> *Say, who else would return the memory of life*
> *To men with a torn hope?"*

It is the Negro, who, through his art, shakes off the old European reliance on order and reason and who resorts instead to the magic of the word in order to capture and to fascinate. It is the negro writer who takes possession of the world and recreates it for the benefit of all mankind, through the magic of the word.

The poem, *Cahier d'un Retour au Pays Natal*, has been translated into several languages. It contains the first use of the word, Negritude, and the first brief illustration of the various stages of its development.

The poem starts with a bitter evocation of the poverty of the island, Martinique. All about him the poet sees decay and hopelessness. This evokes in him a strong feeling of disgust. That disgust then passes into an expression of hatred for the white world which has been responsible for all that humiliating poverty. This is symbolized by the 'white death' of Toussaint L' Ouverture.

Cahier d'un Retour au Pays Natal is a personal poem, and yet it is more than that. It is a personal poem in that the poet recounts therein his own experiences and his reaction to those experiences. Then he broadens the philosophy embodied in the poem to embrace the experiences of his race as a whole, and then he propounds the destiny of that race – the Black People.

Césaire, as we remember, had steeped himself in European history, philosophy and thought before he wrote that poem. When he came to write it, however, he discarded everything that he had learned from Europe. All the poets, he confesses, that he had studied, and whose works he so dearly loved : *Mallarme*, *Peguy*, the *Claudel* of *Tete D'Or*, and *Rimbaud* – he said good-bye to them all. He had no intention, indeed, he could not possibly write that kind of poetry. For what he had to say, what he had to describe were occasioned by personal experiences and by the experiences of his race – a history of suffering, of exile, of alienation, degradation, humiliation, exploitation, of brutalities and injustices that demanded of him far more than what was termed simply 'Poetry,' as was known in Europe then, could possibly assist him to achieve. He had, therefore, to invent his own style of poetry in order to do that. He had to fashion his own language in order to give vent to his feelings and those of his race.

The description of the island at the beginning of the poem is very different from what the early travellers and tourist brochures tell us. Very different, also, from what another famous West Indian poet, St. John Perse, has given us. For Césaire, Martinique is not one of those "happy isles" and certainly not the one described by James Anthony Froude either, where, according to Froude, the black people lay all day in the sun waiting for oranges, mangoes, grapefruits and innumerable varieties of plums, apples and bananas, to fall into their laps. Not for Césaire those paradise isles. He introduces a discordant voice as he takes a look at the city where he was born, Forte-de-France:

> *"In this inert city, this desolate mob under the sun,*
> *which has no share in whatever is openly expressed,*
> *affirmed, freed in the full daylight of this*
> *our land. No part in the*
> *French Empress Josephine dreaming high above*
> *the 'nigger rabble,' nor in the liberator frozen*
> *in his liberating gesture of white stone. Nor in*
> *the conquistador. No share in this contempt, this*
> *freedom, this audacity.*
> *At the end of the dawn, this inert city, and its*
> *transparency of*
> *lepers, consumption, famines, of fears hidden in*
> *ravines, fears perched in trees,*
> *fears sunk in the soil, fears drifting in the sky,*
> *accumulations of fears with their dung-heaps of*
> *anguish."*

Who is right? St, John Perse, the white West Indian from the privileged class who would never have gone down to that part of Forte-de-France, anyway, or Césaire? Fanon says that it is Césaire, and he says further Césaire's description is absolutely magnificent. Too realistic, in fact, says Fanon, for it to be called Poetry. One could almost call it somber lyricism, is Fanon's final comment.

That realism is to be found in most of the works of the West Indian writers. We only have to look at the view of life of the dispossessed, but not disenchanted poor of the shanties of Kingston, Jamaica, presented by Roger Mais, to realize how truthful those writers can be. We cannot wonder that when Roger Mais supplemented his fiction with facts at his political rallies, the British Colonial government clapped him in prison. We may call Emile Zola a realist, but when we compare some of his best works with Mais's *The Hills Were Joyful Together*, we have to give Mais the head start.

Here is what Césaire has to say of the house and the street where he lived :

> *"At the end of the dawn, another tiny*
> *house stinking disgustingly in a little narrow street,*
> *a miniature*
> *house which lodges in its guts of rotten wood*
> *dozens of rats, as well as the turbulence of my six*
> *brothers and sisters, a tiny cruel house whose*
> *intransigence drives insanity into our last days*
> *of the month*
> *and my temperamental father gnawed by a certain*
> *ailment, I never discovered what, my father whom*
> *an unpredictable sorcery now makes drowsy with*
> *melancholy tenderness or exalts him to the high flames of*
> *anger; and my mother, whose legs in the service*
> *of our tireless hunger pedaling, pedaling day and*
> *night, I am awakened at night by the rough punctures*
> *in the soft flesh of the night made by the*
> *Singer machine my mother pedals, pedals for our*
> *hunger by day and by night.*
> *At the end of the dawn, beyond my father, my*
> *Mother, the chapped and blistered hut, like a blighted*
> *peach-tree, and the thin roof, patched with bits of tin from*
> *petrol-cans, and this makes swamps of rust in the*

THE LITERATURE OF REVOLT

sordid grey stuff of stinking straw, and when the
wind blows, like the crackling of frying fat
first, then like a burning
log plunged in water with its smoke and embers....
And the bed of boards which brought forth my
race, the whole of my race from this bed of
boards with feet of kerosene cans, as if it
had elephantiasis, this bed with goat-skin
cover and dried
banana leaves and its rags, a nostalgia of a
mattress, this bed of my grandmother (above the bed,
in a pot full of oil, a wick whose flame dances
like a big black beetle, And on the pot in gold letters:
(THANKS)
And a shame, this Rue Paille."

That kind of description of Martinique, and the other islands of the Caribbean we never have had from the white West Indian writers. At least not from St. John Perse, nor José-Maria de Heredia; nor from Le Conte De Lisle, nor the white Jamaican poet, Edward Lucie-Smith. And that is not to say that the Negro is the only race to have suffered, nor alone lives in the slums.

Dostoyevsky's *The House of the Dead*, is horrifying enough. In Henry Roth's *Call It Sleep*, we get some awfully harrowing experiences which the newly-arrived Jewish emigrants undergo in the slums of New York, and the Poles in Nelson Algren's *The Man With The Golden Arms*, or Willard Motley's condemnation of society's inattentions to men like the Italian, Nick Romano, in *Knock On Any Door*.

Those people, however, can, and do escape; one gets the impression that they will get by later on; that those harrowing experiences are merely the initial stages of a re-adjustment in a new land. But what is there, for example, for Bigger Thomas in Richard Wright's *Native Son*? Or in South Africa for the people who inhabit the world portrayed by Ezekiel Mphalele's *Down Second Avenue*? None.

That is what makes Césaire's work so interesting, what compels our attention. For Césaire, having taken a look at the condition of his people, suddenly brings us up sharp with the information that it is not for them alone that he has elected to fight, but, in reality, for humanity as a whole.

Before he can accomplish his ambition, however, to change the world, and to avoid himself falling into that dungeon of despair, there is one thing for him to do, and with one single word Césaire states it: "PARTIR," to flee. To flee, yes, but for a purpose; so that he can equip himself for the coming struggle which he has resolved to take on almost single-handedly. To acquire that knowledge he knows he will have to suffer, that he will have to experience the pains of all mankind. As Professor Guberina had observed "Il (Césaire) faut descendre en enfer pour se purifier.' So Césaire vows to take on the pains of all mankind, for he says:

> "As there are hyena-men and leopard-men, I would
> be a jew-man,
> a kaffir-man,
> a hindu-man-from-Calcutta
> a man from-Harlem-who-does-not-vote ... "

In experiencing those things he would have discovered the power of words, words that will be his devastating weapons:

> *"I should discover once again the secret of great communications and of great combustions. I should say storm. I should say river. I should say tornado. I should say leaf. I should say tree. I should be wet with the rains, made damp with all dews. I should roll like frenzied blood on the slow current of the eye of words like mad horses, clots of fresh children, curfews, vestiges of temples, precious stones far enough away to discourage miners. Whoever would not comprehend me would not Comprehend the roaring of the tiger."*

Brave resolutions, indeed! But first he must get rid of all his acquired European values, and in a famous passage Césaire goes about systematically destroying those values, a spiritual destruction which symbolizes the weapons which the black people of the future will need in order to sever their chains. Césaire hits the nail on the head, so to speak, when he launches his attack upon European Reason, that very Reason in the name of which Europe had so arrogantly assigned to itself the right to designate the Blacks as a 'pre-logical' people. Then Césaire says, rather ironically: Alright, so we are Blacks and that is how you see us; that is how you define us. Very well, then, I accept;

I accept all that you have chosen to say about us. And on behalf of his race he confesses to all the crimes which the Whites have levelled against them:

"I know my crimes; there is nothing to be said in my defence.
Dances. Idols. Backsliding. Me too.
I have assassinated God with my laziness with my
words with my gestures with my obscene songs.
I have carried the plumes of the parrot, the skin
of the musk-rat
I have exhausted the patience of the missionaries,
Insulted the benefactors of humanity,
Defied Tyre. Challenged Sidon.
Worshipped Zambezi.
The extent of my perversity confounds me!"

Then Césaire laughs mockingly at the Whites, and says: 'Take me as I am. I won't accommodate myself to suit you!' (Accommodez-vous de moi. Je ne m'accommode pas de vous!)

Those are fighting words, indeed, and they are meant to announce Césaire's declaration of war in earnest on a Europe which, he says, is "wracked with lies," a Europe which wallows in its "silent currents of despair," a Europe which "over-estimates itself."

Césaire then recalls all the sufferings of the black people, the crushed revolts, the agony and the rivers of blood, and he utters a cry of lament:

"How much blood in my memory. In my memory are lagoons! They are covered with death's heads. They are not covered with water lilies. In my memory are lagoons. No sashes of women on their banks. My memory is encircled with blood. My remembrance Is girdled with corpses."

The remembrance of all those centuries of sufferings and accumulated humiliations jolts Césaire into a brutal awakening. This awareness of his Blackness, his Negritude, strengthens him, intoxicates him. He clothes himself in the grandeur of his past, a past that was once virile, and with all the virile virtues of all those Blacks who had resisted White domination, exploitation and oppression. At that stage it was an abstract blackness, an abstract Negritude in which he luxuriates. The reality was to follow.

Césaire realizes, however, that it is not enough to conjure up glories of the past, for that will not help him, nor the black people's present distress. He admits that, in conjuring up that past greatness of the black people, he had gone to the wrong sorcerer. He shakes himself out of that stupor, and says: "What madness in my dreams of a marvellous caper above this present basement!"

Here, also, Fanon agrees with him, for Fanon says that that will not help in the struggle, that conjuring of the past greatness. We have to deal with the present, and the future. It is not good enough to shout the glory and the grandeur of the past civilizations of the Blacks. And Césaire admits that his cries, those cries of exaltation of that glorious past, his spectacular exorcism, will not be heard by the millions of his black compatriots who still remain enmeshed in, and brain-washed by the accumulated dung of lies put out by Europe. He must, then, give up all that boasting about a race once covered in glory and splendour and face up to the reality of the present, a present that is painful. So he admits all that they have never been, and that their "only incontestable achievement has been the endurance record under the lash."

In the face of that incontestable reality of his history, Césaire bows, and says: "So be it; that's us."

He then relates his experience in Paris which brought him face to face with another reality.

One day on a train in Paris he sees a negro sitting opposite to him, and Césaire says that that man was a hideously ugly Negro. He looked miserable and was badly clothed—a vagabond by all accounts. His gigantic feet which he was trying to hide from the gawking onlookers, and his trembling hands told the story of a hungry boxer. The French women on the train laughed at the ugly, comic Black, and Césaire admits that he was ashamed at that encounter. He saw there a reflection of himself, of his race, and when the women laughed he had to face that reality.

"How farcical my heroism," he says, for he, too, was a black man in that foreign city. He also admits that that encounter and the revulsion which it evoked in him, did, in fact, do him some good. Here he was, the Chevalier of his race, a man pretending to be a rebel, a man who had said that he would defy the white man, and his encounter with another Black who had been reduced to almost nothing, showed him that he could never escape his own personal reality. He could never hide behind a stupid vanity. He says, sorrowfully: "Destiny called to me" and he was hiding behind it.

From that moment Césaire resolved upon his true objective, for he understood then, better than ever before, the sufferings and humiliations of his race, and no longer in abstract terms, either. The true humanity of his people, he recognized, lay not in pride, nor vanity, neither in the capacity to tame the world; nor in the grandiose revolts which, the poet, was advocating and about which he was singing. The true humanity of his people was to be found in all 'that land of suffering' whose every minute recesses the old slave had explored; in the ancestral values which they had managed to preserve, despite their exile and enforced servitude. It is to be found, also, in their capacity to understand the world intuitively, to adapt to the world rather than to try to dominate and to rule it, and in that contact with the cosmic forces which they had never lost, the symbols and myths of the black people. Those were more important than the white world's achievements which had only resulted in the dehumanization of the Whites themselves.

Césaire then considers the special contribution which the black people bring to the world. They had found their true place in the world, but he had first to delve into his Negritude and to propound the concept of that Negritude. Inspired by that he then took unto himself the responsibility of being the spokesman for his race before the bar of humanity. Solemnly he dedicates himself to the task of rousing his people from their stupor, to defend them against all attacks, and to make them send forth their special message, their special radiance to illuminate humanity as a whole. But first he must free himself from all forms of hatred:

> *" ... my heart, preserve me from all hatred do not make of me that man of hate for whom I feel nothing like hate for although I have set myself down in this unique race you know, however, my tyrannical love, you know that it is not out of hatred for other races that I have chosen to labour for this unique race that what I want is for universal hunger for universal thirst."*

Thus has Césaire defined and described the successive stages in the development of his black consciousness, his Negritude. His experiences have evoked pity in himself and he wants now to aid all the damned of the earth. He does not wish to confine himself anymore solely to the black people. His youthful idealism enthuses him with the desire and the determination to take up the cause of all the oppressed peoples of the world, "tous les deamnés de la terre; tous les opprimés du monde." Because that is the only way to have peace and a reasonable security in this world.

He will be the hero of all those oppressed peoples; the one who will be their bard. Having delved deep to find his rightful place, his proper roots amongst his people, Césaire feels that by that "descent into hell," to quote Jean-Paul Sartre in his comparison of Césaire with Orpheus, he will be enabled to save, to liberate the entire black race.

He refuses to shrink from that task, and he says: "J'accepte ... J'accepte entièrement, sans réserve ... "

With that acceptance of his responsibility, that total identification of the poet with his race, Césaire feels that he can make known to the world, can now offer his services, in fact, on behalf of mankind as a whole. He has rid himself of the old Negritude, the old Uncle Tom Negritude, the old Negritude of the "good" Negro. That old Negritude is dead. And for that Césaire says "Hurrah!" That old Negritude which used to say to the white people "Look, I can bow and scrape like you, like you I can pay compliments, in short, I am no different from you; pay no attention to my black skin, it is the sun that has burnt me." That old Negritude is dead, and Césaire says, let us say farewell to that. Then, finally, in a famous passage which, without question, can be considered the finest piece of all, Césaire makes that gesture of love and tolerance, that declaration of supreme optimism to all mankind to join with him and his race in the building of that unique world where all will share in the finest victory of all—the victory of human dignity. Here it is :

> *"We are standing now, my country and I, hair in the wind, my little hand now in its enormous fist, and force is not in us, but above us, in a voice which pierces the night and the audience like the sting of an acopolyptic hornet And the voice declares that for centuries Europe has stuffed with lies and bloated us with pestilence, for it is not true that the work of man is finished that we have nothing to bring to the world, that we are parasites in the world that there is nothing more for us to do but to fall in step with the rest of the world but the work of man is only just beginning and it remains for man to conquer all the violence hidden in the recesses of his passion and no race*

possesses a monopoly of beauty of intelligence, of force and there is a place for all of us at the rendezvous of victory....."

That is the philosophy which Césaire has propounded, the Philosophy of Negritude, and which has so often been misunderstood by the white world. It is not racialism, the criticism that has often been levelled at Césaire, a criticism that has caused Senghor, the other great exponent of Negritude, and a protégé of Césaire, to come several times to Césaire's defence. Negritude, Senghor had often repeated, is not racialism, but humanity.

Je dis hurrah ! Le vielle négritude progressivement cadavérise l'horizon se défait, recule et s'élangit et voici parmi des déchirements de nuages la fulgurance d'un signe le négrier craque de toute part….Son ventre se convulse et résonne ... L'affreux ténia de sa cargaison ronge les boyaux fétides de l'étrange nourrison des mers d'entendre la menace de ses grondisments intestins."

Aimé Césaire

(I say hurrah! The old Negritude progressively disintegrates, the horizon breaks, recedes and expands and here among the tatters of clouds the flashing of a sign the slave galley crumbles…Its belly convulses and growls…The frightful tapeworm of his cargo gnaws the fetid guts of the strange nursling of the sea! And neither the joyfulness of sails swollen with a pocketful of doubloons, nor the tricks played on the dangerous folly of policing frigates can prevent it from hearing the threat of his intestinal rumblings.)

CHAPTER 4
The Flashing Sign

WE SAW HOW THE WRITERS, HAVING TURNED THEIR backs on Europe, chose to exalt what was peculiarly their own. For the first time in Caribbean literature we hear the throbbing of the drums, the gentle caressing of the guitars, the trembling of the maracas, the wild abandon in the movements of the dance, the rum drinking, the violence, the sheer animalism of sexual love, the magic and the captivating mysteries of Voodoo and Shango ceremonies. We hear, for example, the Puerto Rican poet, Luis Pales Matos, addressing the god, Ogun "Who shines in Voodoo With his spurs and saber" and Edward Brathwaite invoking the Voodoo god, Legba, to open the door so that the ceremony can commence:

"Att
Att
Attibon
Attibon Legba
Attibon Legba
Ouvri bayi pou' moi
Amen
Ouvri bayi pou' moi."

In the dance movements and Caribbean rhythms no one has captured their substance more beautifully than Cuba's Nicolas Gullen and, in so doing, reached directly into the heart and soul of the people.

Those writers had identified themselves with what they knew and understood well, and some of those things were what Europe had objected to and had tried to eradicate. Now Europe was forced to listen.

Césaire had given a firm base for the rehabilitation of Negro culture in the Philosophy of Negritude. To-day that philosophy lives on, even though under a different banner – Creolité or Antillanité – by a new generation of writers in Martinique and Guadeloupe. The writers to-day, as with those in the past generation, have sought not an overthrow of all the inherited cultural values and to replace them with African, but rather, their insistence is in a re-examination by calling into question the arrogance of the European in thinking and believing that his was the only valid and worthwhile culture, and to call the black and the brown people of the Caribbean to a revaluation of the African cultural elements in their society, and in African civilization as a whole.

That movement in thinking, although it gained force in the 1930s, actually began in Haiti in the eighteenth century when the slaves rebelled and defeated the European armies. It continued in Haiti when the United States of America landed her marines in that country. The effect of that occupation was to make the people sceptical about the intentions of the United States, for it smacked too much of Big Brother wielding the big stick. The other effect was to make the Haitians turn inward, that is, to look at themselves. Dr. Jean Price-Mars must be given credit for that inward look. Dr. Price-Mars went about the country collecting the people's folklore which they had brought with them from Africa, and telling them, in effect, to forget Europe and North America and to value those things which were their own. Dr. Price-Mars was supported in that endeavour by ten other Haitian intellectuals, one of whom was Dr. Francois Duvalier, 'Papa Doc.'

It is true that, in the main, West Indian writing did not follow any tradition. There was a body of men, however, who grew up and followed in the path of Western European thought. They were the men who had cleared the deck, so to speak, for the moderns. Men of the calibre of John Jacob Thomas, Alfred Mendes, C.L.R. James, Marcus Garvey, George Padmore, and others. They had studied Western European history, Western European literature, Western European philosophy, and the origins of their works and thought were to be found in those. What those men had become, then, was the direct result of what they had learned and understood about themselves from having immersed themselves in the tenets of Western civilization.

They mastered the literature, history, philosophy and ideas of Western Europe, and in so doing, gained an understanding of themselves, of black people, and of all the deprived, colonized, oppressed and dispossessed peoples of the world. When they spoke and wrote they not only excelled their masters, they also frightened them.

Let us get acquainted with some of them. Many of them were

white, or brown, and came from the privileged class, but they were all West Indians, and had taken up the struggle on behalf of the underprivileged West Indians. Some had never seen the inside of a university, but they had that avid desire to know and to understand the world about them and the West Indian predicament.

John Jacob Thomas was born in 1840, just six years after emancipation, thus his parents had been slaves and, no doubt, must have been undergoing the period of indenture after emancipation which the Planters and the British Government had devised in order to keep the former slaves tied to the plantations. Late in his life John Jacob Thomas started to write a history of the emancipation of the slaves, but died before the book was completed. He did write two books, *The Theory And Practice Of Creole Grammar* (1869), and *Froudacity* (1889), a riposte to James Anthony Froude's Negrophobia: *The English in the West Indies, or The Bow of Ulysses*. Froude was, at the time, Regius Professor of Modern History at the University of Oxford. John Jacob Thomas was a schoolmaster in Trinidad.

James Anthony Froude, a friend of Thomas Carlisle, an anti-Black writer and politician, visited the West Indies and wrote his book attacking the ex-slaves, saying that slavery ought never to have been abolished. The book created an immense amount of ill-feeling in the West Indies, and Thomas went into the attack with his reply to Froude in *Froudacity*.

West Indians, as has been shown, cannot tolerate injustice and will take issue with anyone who is foolish or careless enough to imagine that he can take liberties with them. Thomas took up Froude's audacity point by point and did a thorough demolition job on this Oxford Professor and hater, not only of Blacks, but of the Irish as well. Catholics, according to Froude, was such an abomination that it was not even a sin to kill one. Wrote Froude:

> *"If we extend to Ireland the independence which only links us closer to Australia, Ireland will use it to break away from us. If we extend it to Bengal, and Madras and Bombay, we shall fling them into anarchy and bring our empire to an end. We cannot for our safety's sake part with Ireland. We do not need to part with our Asiatic dominions. The reality of the relation in both cases is the superior force of England, and we must rely upon it and not try to conceal that we do, till by the excellence of our*

administration we have converted submission into respect and respect into willingness for union."

For the West Indians Froude did not mince words either. He sounded only too sorry that slavery had been abolished.

"Slavery was a survival from a social order which had passed away, and slavery could not be continued. It does not follow that per se it was a crime."

His view of the Negroes was that:

"The Negroes of the West Indies are children, and not yet disobedient children. They have their dreams, but for the present they are only dreams."

Thus their dreams being merely the dreams of children the West Indians must never therefore be given any form of self-government. They will never be able to Govern themselves.

"The West Indian negro is conscious of his own defects, and responds more willingly than most to a guiding hand. He is faithful and affectionate to those who are just and kind to him, and with a century or two of wise administration he might prove that his inferiority is not inherent, and that with the same chances as the white he may rise to the same level."

That is not all that Froude had to say about them. He continues:

"The poor black was a faithful servant as long as he was a slave. As a freeman he is conscious of his inferiority at the bottom of his heart, and would attach himself to a rational white employer with at least as much fidelity as a spaniel."

John Jacob Thomas did not attend any university. He had not read Voltaire, Rousseau, Plato, Cicero or Aristotle, but his logic was pure, his command of language perfect, and his analysis of events revealed his strong sense of history. Froude had started with the assumption that the West Indian Blacks were inferior beings. Thomas, six years away from slavery, goes into the attack:

> "It sounds queer, not to say unnatural and scandalous, that Englishmen in these days of light be the champions of injustice towards their fellow subjects, not for any moral or intellectual disqualification, but on the simple account of the darker skin of those who are to be assailed and thwarted in their life's career and aspirations. Really, are we to be grateful that colour difference should be made the basis and justification of the dastardly denials of justice, social, intellectual, and moral, which have characterized the regime of those who Mr. Froude boasts were left to be the representatives of Britain's morality and fair play? Are Negroes under the French flag not intensely French? Are the Negroes under the Spanish flag not intensely Spanish? Wherefore are they so? It is because the French and the Spanish nations, who are neither of them inferior in origin or the nobility of the part they have each played on the historic stage, have the dignity and sense to understand the lowness and or moral and intellectual consciousness implied in the subordination of questions of an imperial nature to the slave-holder's anxiety about the hue of those who are to be benefited or not in the long run. By Spain and France every loyal and law-abiding subject of the Mother Country has been a citizen deemed worthy of all the rights, immunities, and privileges flowing from good and creditable citizenship. Those meriting such distinction were taken into the bosom of the society which their qualifications recommended them to share, and no office under the Government has been thought too good or too elevated for men of their stamp. No wonder, then, Mr. Foude is silent regarding the scores of brilliant coloured officials who adorn the civil service of France and Spain, and whose appointment, in contrast with what has usually been the case in British Colonies, reflects an abiding lustre on those countries, and establishes their right to a foremost place among nations."

Thomas reminded Froude that the emancipation of the Blacks in the United States of America was forced upon the Whites by necessity, and that "No abstract principle of justice or of morals was of primary consideration in the matter."

When Froude said that slavery had been beneficial to the Blacks because in their own African countries they would have been slaves receiving worse treatment, Thomas was only too happy to remind him that such a statement was false, and "in the face of the facts which could not possibly have been unknown to him, a piece of very daring assertion. But this should excite no wonder, considering that precise and scrupulous accuracy would be fatal to the discreditable cause to which he so shamelessly proclaims his adhesion." Thomas adds further that:

> *"As being familiar since early childhood with members of almost every tribe of Africans (mainly from or arriving by way of the West Coast) who were brought to our West Indies, we are in a position to contradict the above assertion of Mr. Froude's, its unfaltering confidence notwithstanding."*

Concerning the only kind of slavery known in Africa in "those patriarchal ages" when slaves were bought, Thomas tells Froude that "The slaves so purchased, we know, became members of the families to which their lot was attached, and were hedged in from cruel usage by distinct and salutary regulations." Very different, in fact, from the type of slavery which the Europeans had instituted in the West Indies.

Thomas wrote another book, *The Theory And Practice Of Creole Grammar,* which was published in 1869. He was one of the first to make a thorough study of Creole and to recognise it as a language, regarding Creole in the same parallel as "the development of the Romance languages from their Latin stem after the Roman Empire had broken up and barbarian peoples had begun to remould Latin according to their own verbal rhythms." Thomas went to London in 1873 where he read a paper 'On Some Peculiarities of the Creole Language.' before the Philological Society. Later he was made a member of the Society.

The tradition of this study of Caribbean folk languages, dances, beliefs and proverbs was continued at the beginning of the twentieth century by Dr. Jean Price-Mars of Haiti, of whom we shall now consider.

For most of the one hundred and fifty years after the Haitian slaves had fought for and had won their independence from France, Spain and Britain, Haiti remained isolated from the rest of the world. The Great Powers of the day had seen to that, had ensured that no one went to Haiti's aid. There was no body of nations such as the League of Nations in the 1920s, nor the United Nations of to-day to which the Haitians could turn or to appeal for help. Fidel Castro was more fortunate than the early Haitian leaders of the eighteenth and nineteenth centuries. Britain was the only country which came forward, but it was merely to deceive the Haitians, as we shall see later, in order to get her own back on France.

The action by Britain inadvertently drove the Haitians on to an historical course which Europe has no right now for which to condemn the Haitians.

Sainte Dominique (Haiti) was the richest prize in the world of the slave era, and she was a colony of France. Without her and the wealth she provided the French, France would have collapsed long before the steady and repeated onslaught of the British army and navy. Haiti went, and the British rejoiced.

Toussaint had been removed, and when Lelerc wrote to Napoleon that it was not enough simply to remove Toussaint for there were 2,000 others to take his place, Napoleon knew that he had a fight on his hands.

Dessalines had taken over from Toussaint and had won the war against France, but Britain had sleepless nights. What if Haiti and France were to come to some rapprochement, as seemed likely, once France had seen that she could never subjugate those former slaves? France would then become again the greatest economic force in Europe, and the world, even. Britain was determined, therefore, that the break with France be made permanent and irrevocable.

Britain intimated to the Haitians that France was secretly planning another invasion of the island in order to restore slavery. The Haitians had fought a war that had lasted twelve years; they were tired and exhausted. All they wanted was to be left alone so that they could restore the country's wealth and to live in peace; to be able to trade with North America and Europe.

The Haitians sincerely believed the British when they told them that Britain alone could be depended upon to guarantee Haiti's safety. At a meeting with the Haitian leaders in December 1804, the English representative, Colonel Cathcart, along with two others, informed the Haitians that they would be prepared to protect Haiti from the coming French invasion, and would trade with Haiti, but only after the last of the Frenchmen on the island had been killed.

Dessalines had seen many horrifying things during that twelve years war. It had been the worst of all wars up to that time, a racial war of indescribable atrocities. Yet such had been his mood of reconciliation that he had even restored some of the large estates to their former French owners who had remained on the island. For all we know they would have remained there unmolested. Dessalines had more or less forgotten those Frenchmen and had turned his attention to formulating the first laws for Haiti by which the country would be governed.

Dessalines believed the Englishmen. He had suffered much and he had seen much suffering caused by the Whites. If to prevent the restoration of slavery meant doing what the English wanted, then it had to be.

This is what C. L. R. James had to say about what happened in the new year of 1805:

"The massacre of the whites was a tragedy; not for the whites. For those slave-owners, those who burnt a little powder in the arse of the negro, who buried them alive for the insects to eat, who were well treated by Toussaint, and who, as soon as they got the chance, began their old cruelties again; for these men there was no need to waste one tear or one drop of ink. The tragedy was for the blacks and the mulattos. It was not policy but revenge, and revenge has no place in politics. The whites were no longer to be feared, and such purposeless massacres degrade and brutalise a population, especially one which was just beginning as a nation and had had so bitter a past. The people did not want it – all they wanted was freedom and independence seemed to promise that. Had the British and the Americans thrown their weight on the Side of humanity, Dessalines might have been curbed. As it was Haiti suffered terribly from the resulting isolation. Whites were banished from Haiti for generations, and the unfortunate country, ruined economically, its population suffering from lack of social culture, had its inevitable difficulties doubled by this massacre. That this nation survived at all is forever to its credit, for if the Haitians thought that imperialism was finished with them they were mistaken."

C. L. R. James added: "Pitt, Dundas and the rest were satisfied. The wonderful colony of San Domingo was no longer a rival."

The nature of that bitter and bloody rivalry between England and France in relation to Sainte-Dominque, has been dealt with by

Adam Smith in *The Wealth Of Nations*, in the chapter entitled *Chapter VII – Of Colonies – Part First – Of the Motives for Establishing New Colonies.*'

One may well ask: What has that piece of history to do with literature? The answer is that the economic decay and political disorder which seems endemic in Haiti to this day, started then. Having no one to whom to turn the Haitians turned upon themselves. For fifty years no form of Christianity was practiced in Haiti because no priests were permitted to return to the island. The Haitians, therefore, turned to the only religion that they knew and understood, the one which had sustained them throughout their period of slavery, the religion which they had brought with them from Africa.

Every now and again white writers and white politicians have thrown all sorts of accusations at the Haitians, but we shall look in vain for any mention of the part that Europe had played in that state of affairs. One of those to mock the Haitians was Graham Greene in his novel, *The Comedians*. The man, however, who started the whole anti-Haitian propaganda and all the frightening stories about Haiti, Voodoo, and all the blood-curdling Satanic rites was Selden Rodman with his book *Haiti The Black Republic*. The outside world took its cue from there on and that 'image' of Haiti continues to this day.

The Haitians, however, despite all criticism, managed to retain their independence, without any thanks to the foreign whites who, day after day, year after year, have never left Haiti alone.

Then in 1915, to crown it all, after those years of ceaseless batterings from the Whites in Europe and North America, American marines landed on Haitian soil on some pretext that the Haitians owed money to the U. S. A. Once more the Haitians were threatened. Once again they sought for a rallying point to repel the enemy.

Dr. Jean Price-Mars has described the mood of the Haitian people and how that rallying point was reached, in his book *De Sainte Dominique à Haïti – Essai sur la Culture, les Arts et la Littérature*. The book was written, said Dr. Price-Mars, because at that precise moment in Haiti's history, "il nous a semble opportune de mètre en en évidence ce qu'en 155 années d'indépendance a réalise le people haïtien au point de vue culturel."

Dr. Price-Mars affirms that between 1898 and the 27th. July 1915, the day the North Americans landed, and "une véritable catastrophe s'abattit sur le pays," no white person had ever been molested in Haïti

" ... aucun Américain, aucun étranger, n'avait été molesté dans ses biens ou dans sa personne."

1915 was the first year of the war, and Europe, Dr. Price-Mars reminds us, was plunged into a terrible war with the United States still neutral. He tells us further that "elle (USA) profita de la confusion mondiale pour étendre plus avance des aspirations dominatrice sur les petites nations de l'Amérique latine."

In 1895 the United States of America had taken the side of Venezuela in the frontier dispute between Venezuela and British Guiana, and Richard Olney, the USA's Secretary of State had written arrogantly to Britain's Lord Salisbury, that "To-day the United States of America is practically sovereign of this continent and its fiat is law upon the subjects to which it confines its interpretations." In other words, Britain must "Shut up!" when the USA did anything from then on in that hemisphere. The USA had made it quite clear that whichever side she took or backed, no European power had a right to interfere, or say anything.

Dr. Price-Mars reminds us that the United States had wielded the 'big stick' before in asserting her supremacy by military intervention in Mexico, Nicaragua, Cuba and the Dominican Republic and that it was now Haiti's turn for the "gros baton."

It was one hundred and eleven years ago, Dr. Price-Mars tells us that Haiti had gained her independence "par le fer et par le feu," and though Haitians had painfully served their apprenticeship in the art of self-government, had often made mistakes, nevertheless they had managed to remain on that road which would one day lead them to their veritable goal, even though they may appear to the rest of the world like some drunk who staggers but yet will reach his destination.

American military might, Dr. Price-Mars said, made it impossible for the Haitians to take on the colossus of the North, so "nous nous accrochâmes à la résistance culturelle. Sur ce terrain, nous réalisâmes l'union nationale."

American military might, then, forced the Haitians to look at themselves, to take stock, so to speak. It was during that period that Dr. Price-Mars wrote his famous book, *Ainsi Parla L'Oncle*, (Thus Spake Uncle), and encouraged the formation of societies to perpetuate the African way of life in Haiti and the rest of the Caribbean, and thereby made the peasant the axis of literary creation. He had pointed the way, and to-day we find that almost every first novel by a West Indian writer is about the peasantry. He may discuss the middle class in his second or third book, but he never strays very far from the soil.

According to Dr. Price-Mars, it was in 1928, under the Presidency of Louis Borno that:

"Une violente campagne vigoureusement nationaliste et antiaméricaine, très ans après le débarquement, commence cette année-la, conduit par Jacques Roumain et Georges Petit dans la journal 'Le Petit Impartial.'

The rebellion against the American occupation had begun in earnest and with people being involved being arrested, imprisoned or shot, the first of such persons being Charlemagne Peralte in 1919 and Benoit Batraville in 1920.

Not only the writer Jacques Roumain, but others such as Jean Stephen Alexis with his novel *Les Arbres Musiciens* and *L'Espace D'Un Cillement.*

Hans Schmidt in his book *The United States Occupation of Haiti,'* says that the USA had sent marines into Haiti in 1915 because of fears that Germany might establish submarine bases there and that would have threatened American shipping and the Panama Canal. The marines, however, remained long after the war had ended, and that for other reasons, among those being that the USA wanted to prevent any attempt to overthrow the Haitian regime that had been put into power by the USA; also, to guarantee long-term American financial interests in that country.

What really transpired was that the occupation forces got progressively more involved in Haiti's internal affairs: dissolving legislatures, manipulating elections and, worst of all, introducing and practicing an effective blatant racial discrimination and racial segregation. Even special segregated masses were conducted for Americans. In addition, getting engaged in guerrilla warfare and rounding up Haitians for forced labour. The Haitians violently resented that racial segregation in their own land.

As Richard Colney, the USA's Secretary of State had said, the USA would do whatever it liked in the Caribbean, and that same policy of intervention was continued in the Dominican Republic, in the attempted invasion of Cuba and the subsequent Bay of Pigs fiasco, and in the 1970s, the invasion of Grenada in the Windward Islands after the death of Prime Minister Maurice Bishop.

Until the invasion of Haiti and the occupation, Haiti's societal construct was based on race and lightness of complexion, with the élite, almost all Mulattos, persisting in copying and imitating everything from Metropolitan France – social mannerisms, intellectual and cultural refinements, and an insistence on the French language as a mark of sophistication and a repudiation of the African heritage of the majority black population. Even a worse practice was that the Americans, during the occupation, favoured Mulattos in their choice of Presidents and in the major Cabinet posts.

The reaction of the Haitians to all this was a rejection of North American and European culture, first by the Blacks and later, also, by the Mulattos. With the publication of his book *Ainsi Parla L'Oncle*, by Dr. Price-Mars, the search for an indigenous black cultural heritage began. The movement, which was known variably as 'L'Indigénisme' and 'L'Haitienisme,' and 'L'Africanisme,' sought to glorify black folk culture (folklore, religion and the Creole language). Poets and novelist joined in the attack. Those writers who, previously, had copied or imitated French literary styles, now took on a strong social orientation and dealt mainly with the Haitian peasants and their black African heritage.

The Haitians had found their rallying point in their own backyard, had discovered themselves in the lives of the peasants who had never deserted Africa. They said good-bye to the Marseillaise and began to take pride in their own customs and beliefs: their family relations, their social practices, their drums, songs, music, whatever they remembered of the arts which they had brought with them from Africa. Above all, they turned passionately to their own religion – Voodoo.

All those things represented Africa to the Haitians. Africa rediscovered in the Caribbean. Even the Haitian élite were overjoyed; they were now able to say to the devil with Europe and North America.

Under the guidance of their intellectuals the Haitians set about getting rid of the North Americans. The United States finally gave up on their entry into the Second World War, but not before they had extracted from the Haitians the rescinding of that clause in their Constitution which had bothered them for a very long time, and which had laid down that no Whites were to be allowed to own land in Haiti.

Unlike John Jacob Thomas, Dr. Jean Price-Mars had received an excellent education. He was born on the 15th. October 1876, and, like Franz Fanon, studied Medicine, qualifying at the Faculty of Medicine in Paris. From 1899 until his death he was at one time or another, Professor, Rector of the University, Deputy, Senator, Minister Plenipotentiary, President of the Haitian Delegation to the United Nations, Haitian Ambassador to Paris, and he attended numerous conferences in various parts of the world. Science and Culture were his field. In 1956 he was President of the First International Conference of Negro Writers and Artists held at the Sorbonne in Paris. His other works included *Formation ethique, Folklore et Culture,* and *Silhouettes nègres et négrophiles.*

The two other writers, Marcus Garvey and George Padmore, are two of the West Indians concerned primarily with the emancipation of Africa from colonial domination by Europe.

Garvey was the more race conscious. His vehement denunciation of the exploitation, in all forms, of the black people, made him the focal point of all who sought redemption for the black race. Garvey went to the United States and sought to create a new society in Africa for black Americans. In seeking to put his dream into reality Garvey did not make his appeal in any metaphysical language, but in his call for resolute action.

More than forty years later another West Indian, Stokeley Carmichael, from Trinidad and Tobago, sought to achieve redemption of the black Americans on American soil.

Garvey's vision of the salvation of the black people lay in self-reliance and kindness, conscious human endeavour. He called upon the black people to remove the scales from their eyes and seek Negro power, and through that power, freedom, dignity and integrity. His appeal was that of the Black Nationalist, and the force that he set in motion is still very much alive to-day.

Garvey had a tremendous following both in the United States and in the West Indies. His persistent cry was "Wake up, Africa! Let us work towards the more glorious end of a free, redeemed and mighty nation. Let Africa be a bright star among the constellations of nations." Strange as it may seem to-day, that sentiment had come from a West Indian who had never visited Africa, yet he succeeded in conveying to millions of black people throughout the world that Africa was their rightful place and home, and the home of a civilization which had once been great and would be great again.

He was at pains to point out, however, that that would only come about by the concerted endeavour and the resolute actions of the black people:

> *"Those who for four centuries have been the craftsmen of black servitude because they had strength and science at their service, have magnified the adventure by telling that the Negroes were the trash of humanity – without history, without morals, without religion; by telling that they have to be infused no matter how, with new moral values, a new human investiture."*

Black people everywhere seized upon Garvey's words and those black people who had never before existed in the political consciousness of the world suddenly were placed there and have remained there since, never to be removed.

After Garvey came C.L.R. James, H. Sylvester Williams and George Padmore, all of Trinidad and Tobago, who sought to create new societies in Africa through liberation from British imperialism.

George Padmore was one of the greatest fighters for the liberation of Africa. He was the originator of the movement, and he is known to-day as the Father of African Emancipation. He was, without doubt, one of the outstanding West Indians of the twentieth century. When he had completed his education in Trinidad he worked for a time as a journalist in Trinidad. Then he left for the United States, arriving on Ellis Island on the 29th. December, 1924. He studied Sociology at Columbia University before going to Fisk in Nashville, Tennessee, where he had hoped to study Medicine. He changed his mind and read Law instead, and Political Science. In the meanwhile he kept at his Journalism, accepting engagements to speak on various political and allied topics, until gradually he had become one of the most popular and forcefully competent speakers in the USA. On one occasion he appeared on the same platform alongside some famous dignitaries of the academic world to speak on the situation in China. He gave up Fisk and entered New York University.

Padmore's first attack against British Imperialism was launched against Sir Esme Howard who had come to the university to dedicate its International House. Quite apart from being Britain's Ambassador to the United States, Sir Esme Howard had been the man who had been instrumental, according to Padmore, in getting Marcus Garvey deported from the United States. With that attack Padmore's political career was launched.

He wrote without respite and black people read his articles and pamphlets and followed his activities closely. At about that time Padmore joined the Communist Party, having found that that Party was the only group of people willing to deal with the racial dilemma that was slowly engulfing the United States and the rest of the world. Whenever, however, they showed any sign of treating the racial question and the black people as incidental to their world-wide campaign against capitalism and totalitarianism, Padmore attacked them. To him the racial question appeared crucial in the fight against Imperialism and Colonialism. Eventually, he broke with the Communist Party for the same reason. He had recognized how insincere were the Russians when they ordered a cessation of anti-Imperialist work being done in Africa and Asia. He made the reasons for the break quite clear:

> *"This I considered to be a betrayal of the fundamental interests of my people, with which I could identify myself. I therefore had no choice but to sever my connection with the Communist International. I formulated my position quite clearly in a political statement which I submitted to the Comitern Executive, and which was subsequently published by the Negro press, so that my case would be put before my own people."*

The Russians promptly labelled him a "petty bourgeois nationalist deviationist," but that did not bother Padmore in the least, for, he reminded his readers, "no one whose disassociation from the Communist ranks might give rise to any political embarrassment is allowed to make his exit without vilification."

Before that, while in Moscow, he had been feted and had been a member of the Moscow City Soviet, a position which the Russians had always been eager to point out to the Western countries that no Black could ever hope to attain in their countries.

From Moscow Padmore went on to Germany where he continued his work. He organized the First International Conference of Negro Workers which was held in Hamburg in 1930 from the 7th. to the 9th. July. Delegates came from the West Indies, West and South Africa. Even as early as that Padmore had tried to make both Negroes and Asians aware of the fact that the black struggles were connected with the revolutionary movements in Asia. Asia, Africa and the West Indies, he asserted, had demonstrated the growing awareness of the peoples of colour that they were capable of managing their own affairs. Padmore was the first black man, and one of the few politicians in Europe at the time who had warned against the creeping disease of Fascism in Germany. Adolf Hitler had him imprisoned when he, Hitler, came to power in Germany.

Padmore moved to Austria afterwards, but, feeling unhappy there, he moved to London where his real life's work began. The British Special Branch were disturbed at his arrival, but having no grounds on which to make any special kind of charge against him, Padmore was allowed to remain. He was a tireless fighter against Imperialism. Racism in Britain he denounced at every level: housing, employment and other areas. His energies, however, were devoted to the final emancipation of the African continent.

In London he edited newspapers and journals, wrote tracts, articles, books, attended and organized conferences, moved numerous resolutions, harassed the British Labour Party whenever and wherever it deviated from its stated principles on Colonialism, and he attacked the Tories mercilessly for their Imperialism and blatant racialism.

Padmore became sceptical about the British Labour Party in 1938, after the Commission of Enquiry set up by the British Government had reported on the labour disturbances in Trinidad. A Labour Party Trade Unionist, Sir Arthur Pugh, and a member of the Commission, had accepted the verdict of the colonial ruling class against the Trinidad trade unionists, and Padmore realized immediately that black workers could expect no help from the British Labour Party in their struggles for economic and social conditions.

Padmore was even more indignant when Joseph Chamberlain stated quite bluntly that Imperialism meant "a certain racial superiority, suppression of political and economic freedom of other peoples, exploitation of resources of other countries for the benefit of the imperialist countries."

Although he refused to make any contribution towards the war effort, reminding the British that he had been against Hitler all along, even when Hitler "was being supported by the City of London, and when British merchants were flooding Germany with the war goods and munitions wanted," he nevertheless sympathized with the Europeans, agreeing with Aimé Césaire that Europe had contrived its own downfall, and that Hitler was only doing in Europe what the Europeans had until then been doing all along to the non-white peoples of the world.

That racism was nothing new to Britain, even during the war, was clear from Padmore's attack on the BBC which had been in the habit of referring to black people as "Niggers." Soon after Dunkirk when the BBC used the word once more Padmore asked the Corporation to re-examine their vocabulary. The BBC apologized for the first time. Padmore's amusing observation was that the light was darkening over Europe and Aunty BBC and the British nation desperately needed the Blacks no doubt to retire to their countries were Britain to be subjugated, in Churchill's words, by the Nazis.

Padmore formed the International African Bureau and, along with five other West Indians, including C.L.R. James, ran the organization. It was, says C.L.R. James, purely a West Indian organization, and until Jomo Kenyatta and later Kwame Nkrumah joined it, so it remained. The organization's motto was "Educate, co-operate, emancipate. Neutral in nothing affecting the African people" Their journal, which C.L.R. James edited, was entitled *The International African Opinion*, and by all accounts of it was a well produced magazine. Membership of the organization was opened solely to Africans and to people of African descent, but anyone who sympathized with its aims could become an associate member.

The Bureau performed an excellent task in enlightening public opinion in Britain, and in the other European countries which possessed colonies inhabited by black people, about the plight of those countries and the protectorates.

Padmore dominated the Bureau. Not only did he do that, but he also established contacts with all the African nationalists and their movements, and formulated and preached his doctrine of Pan-Africanism.

C. L. R. James who knew him well, and who has written a book about him and Kwame Nkrumah entitled *Nkrumah And The Ghana Revolution,* says:

> "*Padmore shook the dust of the cramping West Indies from his feet in the early 1920s and went to the United States. When he died in 1959, eight countries sent Representatives to his funeral in Ghana; and all assert that in that country of political demonstrations there never had been a political demonstration such as was evoked by these obsequies of Padmore. Peasants from remote areas who, it could have been thought, had never heard his name, found their way to Accra to pay the last tribute to this West Indian who had spent his life in their service ...*

> *NBC made a national telecast of the internment of his Ashes in Christianborg Castle, at which Padmore was Designated the Father of African Emancipation, a distinction challenged by no one. To the degree that they had to deal with us in the period between the wars, many learned and important persons and institutions looked upon us and our plans and hopes for Africa as the fantasies of some politically illiterate West Indians. It was they who completely misconceived a continent, not we. They should have learned from that experience. They have not. The same myopic vision which failed to focus on Africa is now peering at the West Indies."*

That piece provides us with a good introduction to the last of the political writers with whom this chapter will deal: C.L.R. James.

Mr. C.L.R. James, whose name has often been mentioned before, came from Trinidad, and he is another of the political writers who played such a magnificently leading role in the Pan-African movement. Mr. James started as a political activist in the Caribbean between the two world wars, and after the wave of riots which had spread throughout the West Indies. He is not only an historian, but a novelist and literary critic as well. His novel, *Minty Alley* was published in 1936 and has now been re-issued. His critique of Herman Melville's *Moby Dick*, is entitled *Mariners, Renegades and Castaways,* and carries the sub-tile *The Story of Herman Melville and the World We Live in.'*

C. L.R. James has also written *A History of Negro Revolt, Modern Politics*, *Party Politics in the West Indies*, *Beyond A Boundary*, *Nkrumah and The Ghana Revolution*, *The Future In The Present*, *Notes On Dialectics* and *The Black Jacobins.*

For many years Mr. James had carried on a very close examination, and a very lucid interpretation of West Indian society, a society which, as we have seen, was the product of a very unique history.

In his book *Beyond A Boundary*, Mr. James examined the different ways in which Victorian attitudes to morality, dress and literature still remain and still influence West Indian life to an astonishing degree. Even more astonishing is when we discover that those attitudes exist, quite often, alongside contradictory African and West Indian ways of life.

Mr. James' book is one of the finest ever written on cricket. It is a stimulating analysis on the aesthetic of cricket. In the

THE FLASHING SIGN

process of his analysis Mr. James also revealed that in the searching for an indigenous West Indian aesthetic the importance of sports to its culture, as well as songs, dances, music and poetry must be taken into account. In the same way that the ancient Greeks had done.

He suggested further that Cricket in the West Indies is more than a sport. He linked it with the Public School ideology and showed that Cricket has done for West Indian society what the Public School ethic has done for the English. Said Mr. James:

> *"There is a whole generation of us, perhaps two generations, who have been formed by it not only in social attitudes but in our most intimate lives, in fact there more than anywhere else. The social attitudes we could to some degree alter if we wished. For the inner self the die is cast."*

Mr. James, however, went beyond Cricket and English values, associating it to the culture of ancient Greece, and tells us that:

> *" ... In the course of duty and for my own information I have read the classics of educational theory and taken an interest in systems of education. Each suited its time, but I have a permanent affinity with only one, the ancient Greek. When I read that the ancient Greeks educated their young people on poetry, gymnastics and music I feel that I know what that means, and I constantly read (and profit by) the writings by most learned professors of Greek culture, who I am sure don't know what they're talking about."*

Mr. James went on to say that he did not merely play Cricket; he studied it. He analysed strokes, studied types, read the history of the game, its beginnings and how and when it changed from period to period. He read and compared statistic, made clippings. He did more:

> *" ... It was in that way, I am confident, that the Greeks educated themselves on games with their records and traditions orally transmitted from generation to generation. Amateur though I am, I see signs of it in Greek literature, but you must have gone through this yourself to understand them.*

I am more certain of the Greek education because it was only after I left school that I began to distinguish between the study of cricket and the study of literature, or rather, I should say, the pursuit of cricket and the pursuit of literature. I did with the one exactly what I did with the other. I paid no attention to the curriculum."

Cricket and English literature became for Mr. James an inexhaustible passion.

" ... I had it from the earliest days that I remember. The boys in ancient Greece must have had the same. If for them games and poetry were ennobled by their roots in religion, my sense of conduct and of morals came from my two, or rather my twin, preoccupations, and I suspect that it was not too different with a Greek boy."

Mr. James never lost his love for Cricket and English Literature. From the one he learned and cultivated body and mind, self-control, courage; from the other he had caught the basic rhythm of English prose, living according to the best tenets of the best writers of English prose, finding in them the same moralism and some of the same stern attitude to life which was all around him, "tempered, but only tempered, by family kindness."

That was the background of the man who later came to write the finest piece of history ever written about the slave revolution in San Domingo (Haiti). That the book is a classic is beyond question, for *The Black Jacobins* is one of the most profound interpretations and one of the most thorough documentation of an event that really shook the world. For anyone who wishes to understand West Indian history, and more particularly, a West Indian's view of the facts, *The Black Jacobins* is incomparable. Here, for the first time, the White man came to know the Black, not as an inferior being, but one with whom he has to reckon. Before the curtain went down, the leader of that revolt, Toussaint L'Ouverture, a slave and stable attendant, had played and played it well, the part of a great soldier in battle, an incomparable administrator in public affairs, and a humane leader of men.

'Qui et quels nous sommes? Admirable question!.

Aimé Césaire

(Who and what are we? Excellent question!)

CHAPTER 5
Caliban Demands a Hearing

THE QUESTION OF IDENTITY IS ONE OF THE MOST vexing for which both the West Indian Blacks and the Mulattos will need to find an answer — Who am I?

The vigour with which the question is being debated at all levels and in every island, reveals how deep is the West Indian's dilemma. Neither the Whites, nor the Indians nor the Chinese have had to make any such soul-searching. Their language, their religion, whatever aspects of their culture which they had chosen to retain and, the most important of all, their names, belong to them. The Black and the Mulatto can claim none of those as his own. Everything that the Whites had been able to take away from them, they took away, deliberately. By depriving them of their very names, that most sacred and cherished ingredient of their Identity, the Whites had reduced the Blacks to a level lower than that of the beasts. On the Bill of Lading they were designated simply by their port of shipment — Mina, or whatever that port of embarkation happened to have been. His new name were the initials of his Master branded on his chest, back and arms with a red hot iron.

About his new name, however, he could do nothing. Nicolas Guillen, a Cuban Mulatto poet, taunting the Whites in a poem entitled *My Last Name*, asks:

"What is my name? Oh, yes, tell me my name!
Andres? Francisco? Amable?
How you always said
Francisco in Dahomeyan?
In Mandingo how do you say Amable?
No? Were there other names, then?
Tell me the surname then!
Do you know my other name, the one that
Came with me from that enormous land,
The captured bloody last name, that crossed the sea
In chains, which came in chains across the sea?
You have dissolved it in imemorial ink ... "

CALIBAN DEMANDS A HEARING   115

We have seen, according to Ligon's account, how he was made to lose his language, and how he came to acquire a new one, that of the Europeans. It was not his language, but from the very beginning he had to learn to indicate whatever he desired in that alien language. Understandably he found himself confronted with a profound dilemma, one which a poet, Leon Laleau of Haiti, expressed in the following words:

> "*Et ce désespoir à nul autre égal*
> *D'apprivoiser, avec des mots de France,*
> *Ce coeur qui m'est venue du Sénégal.*"
>
> *(And this despair equal to no other*
> *To name, with words from France,*
> *This heart which came to me from Senegal)*

Mr. Derek Walcott, in one of his poems, bemoans the loss of those things which meant so much to the black West Indians. He writes:

> "*We left somewhere a life we never found,*
> *Customs and gods that are not born again,*
> *Some crib, some grill of light clanged shut*
> *In us in darkness and beyond*
> *And in its swaddling cerements we're still bound.*"

Claude McKay, of Jamaica, longs for that which he had lost and which he would like to reclaim. He says in the poem *Outcast*:

> "*For the dim regions whence my fathers came*
> *My spirit, bondaged by my body, longs.*
> *Words felt, but never heard, my lips would frame;*
> *My soul would sing forgotten jungle songs,*
> *I would go back to darkness and to peace ...*"

We can see, then, how the West Indians had turned knowledge of the acquired language to his own advantage, devastating to the Europeans. The language that he had learned was not his own, neither was the name he had been given. What belonged to him, exclusively, was his History. Guy Tirolien, for example, says:

*"Je ne connais que l'histoire dans ma chair
par le feu des fouets
le brûlure des garrots
des fers rouges
et de viol..."*

*(I know only the history inscribed in my flesh
by the fire of whips
the scorching of packing sticks
of red hot irons
and of rape...*

C.L.R. James had warned us in *Party Politics in the West Indies*, that we have yet to hear the last of slavery. Indeed, it constitutes the theme of almost every Caribbean poet. For to write of slavery is to examine the extent to which the Europeans had gone in their strategies to dehumanize the Blacks. To write of the dehumanization of the Blacks is to engage in one of the battles in the revolt of the Blacks repudiating the Europeans' creation of black stereotypes, and the derogatory classification of the Blacks. Not to shy away from that history is to declare a new confidence in himself and his people. Guy Tirolien proclaims:

'Branche vivre arraché à l'arbre motilé,
Je repoussé plus dur sur le sol étranger
car ma race est vivace est beaucoup plus tenace
que l'acacia coriace qui poussé à
Sainte Dominique.'

*(Live branch torn from a mutilated tree
I have grown again even stronger in alien soil
for my race is very much alive and much more
tenacious than the tough acacia that grows in
Sainte-Dominique.)*

That is the authentic voice of the black West Indian poet taking stock of his history and talking about himself. Others had written about him, had attempted to define him, but they had not been of his race, hence they had been unable to feel the depth of his distress, the pain of the uprooting, the chaos, the stifling in the holds of the slave ships, the crack of the whip, the groans of his suffering, the cries of anger, the shrieks of those of his brothers and sisters being thrown into the sea.

How would they have felt, then, the power of meaning in the songs and drum-beats of those who had survived, and whose memories were girdled with corpses? The beginning of Negro History in the West Indies has been lost in the dark mantle of night. Who understood and who recorded what the Blacks experienced, and felt? Only the fleeting clouds. Therefore, as the Cuban poet, Nicolas Guillen has said: "We must learn to remember what the clouds cannot forget."

To do that the black West Indian writer had to retrace his steps. Whatever paths he took that was his concern. If he became confused and lost his way, no one ought to laugh at him. The fact that has to be recognized is that by that search he had served notice of his rejection of the European's definition of him, and that he had set out to redefine himself.

In their suffering in exile and in the exploitation of them, the Blacks turned instinctively towards Africa, the home of the black people. What they saw in the 'backward glance,' whether they called it Guinea, Dahomey or the Congo, to them it was Africa. It existed for them even though it was at the level of the metaphysical. Thus had they separated themselves from Europe and started on the road to a re-definition, and in that re-definition their concern was with their blackness, their Negritude, defined with an emotional depth that drove frightened European critics quickly to condemn the black writers as racialists in reverse.

There were some, however, who did not see Negritude as racism; important among them being Jean-Paul Sartre of France, Madame Lilyan Kestleloot of Belgium, Professor Jahnheinz Jahn of Germany, Petar Guberina of the University of Zagreb, Leopold Sedar Senghor of Senegal, and Thomas Melone of the Cameroons.

No, what the Blacks were proclaiming was something completely different. Let us take the slaves in Haiti, for example.

When, under Toussaint, the slaves in Haiti revolted at the end of the eighteenth century, they had thereby declared their rejection of the Judaic-Christian philosophy and theology in whose name and on whose behalf the Europeans had enslaved, and even butchered them. The Haitians promptly replaced that theology with something that they knew and understood; the worship of the Loas, that hierarchy of Voodoo gods and goddesses linked to the ancient pantheon of Guinea, Dahomey and the Congo. That theology belonged exclusively to them, and, indeed, had helped them to withstand and to survive the indescribable horrors of slavery.

For we must recognize that for what it was – the first step in that re-definition of themselves. They had stated quite categorically, that they were not Europeans.

Who, then, were they? We must also be quite clear about that. Gilberto Freyre had said that those who had survived the Middle Passage and were landed in the West Indies were no longer Africans; they were West Indian blacks who were slaves. A Haitian poet, Regnor Bernard, states what had happened:

*"Gone are the forests where sang and danced
the inspired priestess,
and the hearth of the household gods no
longer is lit,
the sacred adder no longer sleeps on the
mapou branch;
the crocodiles are dead on the river banks;
profaned are the alters of the eternal lamp;
and the Spink moans at the empty desert's
edge.
The Pharaohs are troubled at the heart of the
Pyramids;
and Africa no longer is;
neither its temples
nor its mysteries,
for the priests are dead,
for the traders in Negroes have come,
and the tribes of the Congo, of Dahomey
and the Aradas
have known the bite of chains
and of the whip
and the strangling heat of drifting holds ... "*

Four hundred years of slavery had moved the black West Indians farther away from Africa, although the memory of Africa was still present, expressed in their poetry in a mixture of sadness, love and nostalgia. René Maran of Martinique, experiencing the actual discovery of Africa for the first time, spoke of what those four centuries had done to him. In a letter which he wrote to a friend in

Paris, he said: "I sense that I am on the soil of my ancestors, ancestors whom I reprove because I share neither their primitive mentality nor their tastes, but who are nonetheless my ancestors for all that." Although he took up his pen in defence of the Africans, Maran realized that he was and would always remain a West Indian Black.

Another important statement to have been made on the subject of West Indian identity came from the novelist, Vic Reid of Jamaica with his novel, *New Day*. The novel is important because here, for the first time, was put to rest the argument that the West Indians have no history, that nothing of importance, nothing of any value was ever created in the West Indies, a pronouncement made by James Anthony Froude and which was repeated by Vidia Naipaul, more than a hundred years later.

In the matter of literary history the novel is also important for it was the first time, or rather the first West Indian novel to have been written entirely in dialect.

When we look at the first contention, that the West Indians have no history, no identity, we see, after having put down the novel, that that contention could not possible hold. History is the sum total of a people's experiences, and no people, or no group of people can inhabit any place, any country, Vic Reid maintains, and live through four hundred years of the most horrifying existence, and in the end, say of them that no change had taken place there; that such a people have no history; that nothing was ever crated by them; that they evolved no culture that was distinctly or uniquely their own.

Vic Reid is saying in that novel that in the Caribbean we have a history, and we can view that history, if we so desire, either as that of separate racial groups. But that history, to be of any value, must be seen in its entirety; must not be the separate history of distinct racial groups. That is why he has made the people in his novel, Blacks, Whites and Mulattos, an integral part of that history. They are the people who formed Jamaican and Caribbean society during the four hundred years of that turbulent history.

Vic Reid dealt in that novel with Jamaica, it is true, but Jamaica, Haiti, Cuba, Puerto Rico, Barbados, Trinidad or the Guyanas, in fact, the entire Caribbean, went through the same four hundred years of turbulence and change; the same experience of slavery, disruption, chaos and violence; those were the principal elements introduced by the Europeans into the Caribbean; that was all that they had to offer.

Those were the very elements which went into the making of the West Indians, into creating those unique beings.

At the opening of the novel, *New Day*, Johnny Campbell, a man of mixed parentage, but with so much of white blood in him that he could very easily pass for a White, sits alone in his house on the eve of the re-instating of the Jamaican Constitution in 1944, which had been suspended in 1865, after the Morant Bay Rebellion, and he looks back to 1865 and the whole eighty years of turbulence, bloodshed, suffering and deaths that had brought about that change in the island's history. What was it that started that historical change. A drought?

Because of that drought the people are starving; there is no work, yet they are expected to pay taxes. The Police are brutally hunting down those who do not pay. The people petition Queen Victoria after having petitioned the Governor and discovered the Colonial Administrator to have been totally apathetic towards their suffering. It is not simply one group of people who are suffering, but Black, Brown, Mulatto and poor Whites, some of whom are "barefoot German Whites from Seaforth Town."

> *"Petition after petition goes to Governor Eyre at St. Jago, to the Queen Ministers in London and what comes to us but the Queen's Advice, which says we are hungry 'cause lazy we are. Aie ... the feet began trampling with loudness then!"*

The trampling feet of the hungry, angry men take them to the house where the chief magistrate, Custos, a German, is holding a sumptuous banquet. The men demand to speak to Custos, a man who has no sympathy for the suffering people, and whose sentences on the tax defaulters are heavy in the extreme. Custos refuses to see the men's leaders, Paul Bogle. In his arrogance Custos refers to the assembled company as scum and orders the Inspector of Police to order them away. Bogle reminds Custos that he and his men are not scum, but "Free men we are now and loyal subjects to Missis Queen. We must ha' speech with the Vestry."

One man, however, does not take Custos Aldenburg's insult so sedately. "Is who it you call scum, Aldenburg? Is who it?" Others take up the cry and soon the people are shouting and pressing forward. Someone throws a stone which lands upon a Constable's helmet. Then more stones fly through the air. Custos reads the Riot

Act. The first volley from the muskets is directed above the men's heads to frighten them, and because no one was seen to fall, the cry goes up: "Blank! Blank cartridge! They can no shoot down free people!" Once more they demand to see Custos Aldenburg, but he is unmoved. When the muskets sound again this time people fall. When the dust settles and the people disperse forty are left behind dead.

The hungry people did not want war, but they resolve not to allow the deaths to go unpunished. Back in his district Bogle addresses his men and tells them: "Men o' Stony Gut hear me! War is here to-day-to-day."

So once again the bullhorn sounds, the bullhorn which, over the years, had sounded time and again to tell of the numberless slave revolts. Bogle intends to kill only forty of the enemy, so forty for forty is the battle cry.

What transpired, however, became one of the saddest episodes in the sad history of slavery and colonialism in the Caribbean. Governor Eyre let loose the British troops upon the Jamaican population. They hounded, arrested, shot at random and hanged people indiscriminately, often without any trial and regardless of whether or not the people concerned had been involved in the rebellion. The Commission of Enquiry set up by the British Parliament to investigate the massacre estimated that four hundred and thirty-nine Jamaicans had been killed by the British soldiers upon Governor Eyre's instructions. Says Andrew Salkey in his long poem *Jamaica*:

> "Eyre who did give him blessed name to one Australian lake, one Australian peninsular an' a Jamaican genocide."

The island's Constitution is suspended, representative government is withdrawn and Jamaica reverts to Crown Colony government. In the political controversy which followed in England, most of the English intellectuals supported Eyre. The Commissioners themselves were unable to understand why a family such as the Campbells, almost white, came to be involved at all. Campbell had made himself quite clear to his own wife when he told her that "Stoney Gut people are my people" and that "Things have happened to-day, things which must make a man think." Campbell had also discovered that in the colonies there was one law for the absentee landlords, investors and Colonial Administrators, and another entirely different for the inhabitants.

Campbell controls his temper at the depth of the Commissioners' misunderstanding of the situation in the island. Because the Campbells are wealthy people, they ask him:

> *"The – er – colour of your family made you also – er – well thought of in the community. We even understand that the late Custos had spoken of appointing your father a Justice of the Peace. In other words, the point we are making is that you had everything which make you sympathetic to the – er – rulers of your country. What made you join the rebels of Stoney Gut? "my bro' came erect on the rail. Hear him: 'Your honours, because hunger came to my door and I was no' blind.'"*

They ask for clarification, and they get it:

> *"I will tell you. When my family once locked their door everybody around us, 'cept for the wealthy bukras, hungered. Everybody around me were my people, and when they hungered, hungered me too."*

They appear still not to understand and Campbell has to delve into the history of the peoples of the island. At the end of his long speech he predicts that:

> *" ... time will show that St. Thomas people did not die in vain. That the shells 'fore Custos Aldenburg's country- house were a-talk of a new day. Say that good has come o' this march.*

> *"How so? Representative government will come back to our island one day, one day. And mark me, Your Honours, there will be no buckras making the laws then. But the said poor like whom they have killed, and a Governor of the people will be sitting in St. Jago. For we will ha' learnt that sympathy for the poor must come from the poor. Then who will say that time that St. Thomas people died in vain."*

From Campbell's speech we learn that, although slavery had been abolished and the Constitution suspended, nothing had really changed for the mass of the people, the old white plantocracy was still in control. Above all, the events which precipitated the rebellion revealed how slavery has left its mark on every aspect of the society;

how it manipulates the very attitudes and motives of the islanders. In Jamaica all those things worked towards the 1865 rebellion.

New Day spans the long gap between 1865 and the restoration of the Constitution in 1944, and by its very title not only proclaimed a new day but also expressed a new hope.

Whether that promise will be fulfilled or not, again, we must leave to history. For the man, however, who had been present throughout the events that were shaping the nation, there is only pleasure at the sound of his youthful nephew, Garth, as he, too, declares his belief in the future of possibilities.

> *"They are my people, all of them, regardless of the colour of their skins. We are all Jamaicans – in the sun on high places or in the deep valleys heavy with life! In a land where every prospect would please if we had the chance of handling these prospects as we pleased ... My life is mortgaged to this dream....this dream of seeing our people what they ought to be. My life, whatever I possess, is sold out to this dream."*

That has always been the spirit of the Campbells, white, black and mulatto. So now as the old man sits, waiting for the morning:

> *"Memory is pricking at me mind, and restlessness is a-ride me soul. I scent many things in the night-wind is a-talk of days what pass a gone. But the night-wind blows down from the Mountains, touching only the high places as it comes; so then, 'member, I can remember only those places which stand high on the road we ha' travelled. Such a way my people are a-sing, though! You know they will sing all night to-night so till the east wind brings the morning? Torch-light and long-time hymns, and memory a-knock at my mind. Aie, and then there is tomorrow what I must ha' Faith in."*

With the publication of *New Day* the West Indians were able to look at themselves and at their past in a more positive light. They were able to see that past not as one of passive endurance under the whip lash of slavery, but as one of constant bloody struggles and bitter protests; a past of a multitude of courageous slave revolts and protracted wars to ensure their freedom from slavery. Above all, they were able to see themselves as a people who had discovered some positive values as a result of those four hundred years, values which they were now able to offer to the rest of the world. By focusing attention on the common people, Reid was able to show that these people had a history, and a culture uniquely their own.

Vic Reid had remained at home, but there were others who, in their quest for their 'roots,' in their search for their identity, had turned to Africa, and some of them had even made the journey to that continent. As we shall see with Dennis Williams's *Other Leopards*, the answer they found was incomplete, unsatisfactory.

Other Leopards is written in the first person singular and the narrator at one stage confesses to his failure to identify with Africa. "I pressed on the main gate trying hard to feel – how shall I say? ... this mystic union, this ineffable what's-it, this identity. I can never be reproached, God knows, for not trying."

However, as a "bastard with no past, no history, no memory," he has to try, and he tries because as an African chief had said to him of another bastard whose link with his people had been broken "...no man can live without this link, this moral identity. A man must live in time, it is his nature."

The principal personage of *Other Leopards* is Lionel Froad, a West Indian mulatto who not only dreams of a Negro Africa dazzling and glorious in antiquity, but who actually makes the journey to Africa on an archaeological expedition in the hope of having his dreams confirmed, only to have them shattered by disillusionment. His 'backward glance' takes him 5,000 years in time, and what does he discover? His ancestors in chains even then, being lashed with the whip " ... captives going into slavery, that's what Negro means," says an Arab, Fadalla, a member of the expedition. And Dr. King, the English leader of the expedition, adds reflectively later on to Fadalla, as though he had forgotten all about Froad's presence, "Habit's a curious thing, y'know, isn't it? A mechanism you could call it – a tyrannical necessity. The slavery you've just been talking about is nothing to it, nothing."

Williams's novel is one man's search for his identity. Lionel Froad has begun his search in Africa with no high hopes. He is, in essence, the 'uncommitted African,' as he calls himself. From the opening chapters of the novel we already sense that disorientation. An African later mercilessly drives home the point: "I am the true original thing, pure African. I've never been sold, never been a slave. I've got a name, Mr. Lionel Froad, and a tribe. Now tell me who you are?"

Who is he, indeed? The very name Froad is not his. It could even be symbolical for fraud. This state of mind disturbs him. The tension is heightened by the conflict between Lionel Froad and Dr. Hughie King for whom Froad harbours both admiration and repugnance, love and hatred. Dr. King is insensitive to all Froad's attempts to piece links and theories together in order to give some meaning to his past. So much so that, in the end, Froad is forced into an acceptance of emptiness, a desert-like state of mind. He becomes, in reality, an outcast, a bastard:

> *"Between Europe and Africa there is this desert. How fitting! Between the white and the black this mulatto divide. You cannot cross it, whoever you are, and remain the same. You change. You become, in a way, yourself mulatto – looking both ways. Looking back to the vertical, sideways to the horizontal. Backwards to the old mystery, sideways to the timeless mystery. Back to the will and back to the willing .....ai .....and sideways to the calling, the crucifying, the unspeakable-of, the reed shaken by the wind."*

But Froad cannot cross the dividing line, for he is rejected both by Europe, in the person of Catherine, the white girl with whom he is hopelessly in love, and who refuses to accept him with his Africanness, and by Africa, in the person of the black girl, Eve, whom he rejects because of his European orientation, but to whom he feels compelled to return every now and again, for she is, indeed, feminine, intuitive passion and sensuality.

Neither acceptance nor rejection comes easily to Lionel Froad. He vacillates, hoping for the better of the two different worlds, but in the end he is rejected by both. His one consolation is to continue his search for the concrete and material evidence of that past, that glory that was once there.

The Arab has vested interest in trying to disillusion him. Dr. King does not share Froad's personal and emotional involvement, and in the face of the Englishman's intransigence, his superior intelligence which he flaunts so casually, Lionel Froad begins to lose confidence in himself and what he sees and thinks. In desperation one day he picks up a screwdriver and kills Dr. King, and then flees into the desert. Roaming about the desert we hear him wrestling with his conscience:

"How could anyone know what this man's done to me; this thing's not for judgement; what judge can ever know? 'Well, what sort of answer's that Froad? No one will understand. 'This man's made me condemn myself, who'd believe? What was I to do? That crime's got no name; who ever heard of it? Who'll understand?"

The novel ends with Lionel Froad lost in the wilderness, and going insane. He climbs up into a thorn tree, daubs his naked body all over with mud, presumably to hide his mulatto skin, thus signifying his complete rejection of the European part of himself.

"Now having removed my body and the last traces of it, I am without context clear. Going up this new tree, picking the thorns bare, one by one, I am in a darkness nowhere at all. I am nothing, nowhere. This is something gained."

The need for spiritual transcendence which was imperative for Froad, which he had sought and did not achieve, has been established nonetheless. His personal disillusionment is complete, and he desires now only escape. From Europe and Africa no doubt. In his own words he is now "shadowless," and he says ".....Only remains now to remove my consciousness. This I can do whenever I wish. I am free of the earth ... "

The search for origins has led to complete annihilation, which is, in itself, the reality of self-discovery.

We take up now that awareness, that self-discovery, and to do that we must turn to three principal works of Mr. George Lamming: *In The Castle Of My Skin*, *The Emigrants*, and *Season of Adventure*.

René Maran had stated that four centuries of separation from Africa had done its work. The West Indian Black and the Mulatto would need to look afresh at themselves, to look at their history in order to see and to understand what that history had made of them. "But in doing so, my heart, preserve me from all hatred." With those words Aimé Césaire had began his own examination of that history, and he wished to do so without rancour, without recrimination.

In the search for their Identity, as we have seen, it was important for the West Indian writers of African descent to explore their African past. The next question was: Where do we go from there? The centre that was Africa no longer held, for the white man had put a knife on the things that held the Blacks together, according to the Nigerian novelist, Chinua Achebe, and those things had fallen apart. For the restoration of order, therefore, there was need for the establishment of an Identity, a statement, as it were, of who and what they were.

George Lamming's first novel, *In The Castle Of My Skin*, portrays a West Indian colony in revolt. It is about a boy growing up in the colonial world and becoming aware of his situation in that society. We watch the gradually unfolding of the boy's sensibility and how changes in the life of the village where he lives, affect him. Finally we watch the disintegration of that childhood world as the boy moves through and beyond that world.

Our first impression of the novel is of a community concerned only with itself, and its struggles with nature symbolized by the heavy rains and the devastating floods. The inhabitants are not aware of the world outside their village world. Daily chores, gossips, homes and children and their plots of land are their only concern. Theirs is somewhat of a feudal society with the white man, Creighton, head of the village, and his house on the hill dominating all below and about him. That village world even has its own class structure, with mulatto overseers, policemen, and school teachers forming the middle class, and the mass of the black peasants at the bottom of the social ladder. Indeed, nothing appears to us to have changed, as though emancipation had altered nothing, and that the villagers even accept the order of things as though all had been divinely ordained.

When we see what transpired later, however, we have to make our way back to the beginning of the novel to discover what we had apparently missed; the discordant note which had been struck in the opening chapters, telling us that things were not really all what they had appeared to be.

Looking at the pouring rain, for instance, and at the rising water, the boy narrator had reflected not only upon his own aborted dreams, but upon the fate of the villagers as well:

> "As if in serious imitation of the waters that raced outside, our lives – meaning our fears and their corresponding ideals – seemed to escape down an imaginary drain that was our future. Our capacity for feeling had grown as large as the flood, but the prayers of a simple village seemed as precariously adequate as the house hoisted on water."

We are not surprised, therefore, when later, their vision, having been widened, the villagers are made aware of a new consciousness and decide to change, to challenge what had apparently been the accepted order of things. That awakening, however, introduces a new tension, an unsatisfactory state of affairs. There is a strike and Creighton goes after the strike is over, but the middle class, more ruthless than Creighton, the benevolent feudal colonial lord, creates a new tension in the community. There appears only one way out for people like the boy narrator – emigration. To flee, as Césaire had said of his own situation. The book ends with the boy narrator preparing for embarkation for that adult world outside, and to an uncertain future. Boyhood has ended.

But, what was it that had come into the lives of the villagers to disturb that once accepted order of things? It was the return from the United States of America of the boyhood friend of the narrator, Trumper. Trumper's return awakens the villagers to the awareness of a world outside their village world. More than that, it awakened them to the consciousness of their Identity in that larger world. With Trumper's talk about Race and his experiences in the United State of America, people in the village began to think and to discern how the education system had been designed to keep them in ignorance of themselves and of their history. They begin to question that education. " But if you look good," said the shoemaker, "If you look good, you'll never remember that they ever tell us, 'bout Marcus Garvey. They never even tell us that there was a place where we live call Africa."

Their only knowledge of history was that of the English. When it came to themselves all they had ever been told were half truths. Césaire had complained that "For centuries Europe has stuff us with lies and bloated us with pestilence!" The people were taught, for example, that a great English Queen, Victoria, had freed them from slavery, but what slavery was they were only able to visualize as some kind of jail in which they had been locked up.

"That's what," one of the boys said quickly. "Most of them were locked up in a gaol at the same time in the past. And it would appear that when the great Queen came to the throne she ordered that those who weren't free should become free."

Slavery, they conjecture, must have happened many thousands of years ago, so long ago, in fact, that even the history books did not consider it important any more. Some even doubted that slavery ever existed, and, in trying to make sense of the little bits of knowledge that they had acquired, enmesh themselves in greater confusion.

> *"Thank god nobody in Barbados was ever a slave. It didn't sound cruel. It was simply unreal. The idea of ownership. One man owned another". They laughed quietly. "Imagine any man in my part of the world owning a man or a woman from Barbados. They would forget all about it since it happened too long ago. Moreover, they weren't told anything about that. They had read about the battle of Hastings and William the Conqueror. That happened so many hundreds of years ago. And slavery was thousands of years before that. It was too far back for anyone to worry about teaching it as history. That's really why it wasn't taught. It was too far back. History had to begin somewhere, but not so far back. And nobody knew where this slavery business took place. The teachers had simply said, not here, somewhere else. Probably it never happened at all."*

Trumper's return changes all that and adds a new dimension to their village vision. His description of life in the United States and his contacts with Blacks there, "My people," ushers in a new consciousness. About that new consciousness, of Negro-ness, of sharing a common situation with people of the same complexion elsewhere, Trumper confesses:

> *"I didn't know it till I reach the States,"*

and he vows that, having found it:

> *"I'm gonner keep it till thy kingdom come ... If there be one thing I thank America for, she teach me who my race was. Now I'm never goin' to lose it. Never never."*

The narrator, trying desperately for some comprehension, contends that there are black people in Barbados as well:

> *"I know" said Trumper, "but it ain't the same. It ain't the same at all. 'Tis a different thing altogether. 'Course the blacks here*

are my people too, but they don't know it yet. You don't know it yourself. None o' you here on this islan' know what it mean to fin' race. An' the white people you have to deal with won't ever let you know. 'Tis a great thing 'bout the English, the know-how. If ever there was a nation in creation that know how to do an' get a thing do, 'tis the English. My friend in the States use to call them the great administrators. In America I have see as much as a man get kick down for askin' a question, a simple question. Not here. That couldn't ever happen here. We can walk here where we like if 'tis a public place, an' you've white teachers, an' we speak with white people at all times in all places. My people here go their homes an' all that. An' take the clubs, for example. There be clubs where you and me can't go to, an' none o' my people here, no matter who they be, but they don't tell us we can't. They put up a sign, 'Members Only,' knowin' full well you ain't got a chance o' becomin' a member. An' although we know from the start why we can't go, we got the consolation we can't 'cause we ain't members. In America they don't worry with that kind 'o beatin' 'bout the bush."

Trumper later drives home the point while elaborating the difference between the United States and the British colonial experience, a difference, he emphasizes, that lies in the use of one simple word, 'Negro.' He says that in the United States:

"There ain't no 'man' an' there ain't no 'people.' Just nigger and Negro. 'An' little as that seem 'tis a tremendous difference. It make a tremendous difference not to the whites but to the blacks. 'Tis the blacks who get affected by leavin' out the word 'man,' or 'people.' That's how we learn the race. 'Tis what a word can do. Now there ain't a black man in all America who won't get up an' say I'm a Negro and proud of it. We are all proud of it. I'm goin' to fight for the rights o' the Negroes, an' I'll die fightin'. That's what any black man in the States will say. He ain't got no time to think 'bout the rights 'o man or people or whatever you choose to call it. It's the rights o' the negro, 'cause we have gone on usin' the word the others use for us, an' now we are a different kind o' creature, but we got to see first an' foremost 'bout the rights o' the negro, 'cause it's like any kind o' creature to see 'bout itself first. If the rights 'o man and

CALIBAN DEMANDS A HEARING

> *the rights 'o the Negro was the self same thing, 'twould be different, but they ain't 'cause we're a different kind 'o creature. That's what a simple little word can do, an' 'tis what you goin' to learn sooner or later. You'll hear 'bout the Englishman, an' the Frenchman an' the American which mean man of America. An' each is call that 'cause he born in that particular place. But you become a Negro like me an' the rest in the States an' all over the world, 'cause it ain't have nothin' to do with where you born. 'Tis what you is, a different kind o' creature ... "*

The narrator begins to see things a little more clearly now. He would have liked to have asked Trumper for some further clarification, but it was getting late and he would need to prepare for his departure for Trinidad. That departure, Trumper is convinced, will make a world of difference. He tells the narrator, who had asked for some assurance:

> *"You're one of my people all right, but you can't understand it here. Not here. But the day you leave an' perhaps if you go further than Trinidad you'll learn."*

A critic once remarked of West Indian literature that it is one of a series of good-byes. Good-byes to moments and to people who may never meet again. In *The Castle Of My Skin* ends with the narrator, now grown out of his boyhood, leaving the island.

> *"The earth where I walked was a marvel of blackness and I knew in a sense more deep than simple departure that I had said farewell, farewell to the land."*

The real discovery of Identity, however, is achieved with emigration, as we shall see with Mr. Laming's second novel, *The Emigrants*. It is above all a novel of exile, a theme with which Mr. Lamming is concerned in his two other novels, *Of Age And Innocence*, and *Season Of Adventure*.

Exile, Mr. Lamming asserts, is a universal experience. Jean Paul-Sartre, Andre Malraux, and, above all, Albert Camus, have written about it, arguing that the proximity of our lives to the major issues of our time, demands of us all some kind of involvement. They were concerned with political and spiritual exile, while Mr. Lamming's concern is with exile from tradition, from race. Sartre, Malraux and

Camus, and Mr. Lamming, too, are aware that that sense of exile must lead to action; in other words, involvement. Mr. Lamming dramatizes this most forcefully in his two novels, *Of Age And Innocence* and *Season Of Adventure* where he argues that all must help in the building of the new society, and through that involvement, Identity.

In *The Emigrants*, the experience of exile involves a great deal of suffering, and that suffering, Mr. Lamming believes, is necessary, for he makes one of his characters say:

> *"We got to suffer first and come together."*

The Emigrants takes up the moment of departure of the emigrants on their way to Europe, and treats of the discovery of Identity.

In the first novel we saw how the education system had been so designed to keep the West Indians ignorant about themselves and of their history. Because of that education and the clever administration of the islands by the British, the islanders on the boat have no idea, no suspicion, in fact, that their presence will arouse hostility amongst the natives whom they have been taught from childhood to regard as their friends and co-partners in the multi-ethnic Commonwealth. The West Indians feel, therefore, that they are part of England, in a way that perhaps the men who had been sent to administer the islands had never dreamt, nor had ever intended them to become. The shock of contact on arrival, therefore, is so frustrating that bitterness and animosity almost overwhelm them. They are forced to ask themselves then: "Who are we?" and "What are we doing here?" They must discover their Identity, that is, gain recognition as human beings; prove themselves as West Indians. "If you ask what them want to prove," says one of the characters, "the answer sound a stupid answer. Them want to prove that them is themself."

The West Indians in *The Emigrants* come from various islands, and they are fleeing the economic and social conditions of the area. Some of them have been to Britain before, and one of those, Tornado, says to an assembled company during the voyage:

> *"This blasted world is a hell of a place. Why the hell a man got to leave where he born when he ain't thief nothin', nor kill nobody, an' what is more to go to a place where he don't belong."*

Tornado served in the Royal Air Force during the 1939-1945 war in Europe, and had returned home when he was demobilized, but he is here taking flight with the rest. Whatever differences in their past experience they are all taking flight from something they no longer wanted. "It was their last chance," Mr. Lamming tells us, "to recover what might have been wasted,"

From the early conversation of the emigrants during the voyage we gather that they know very little about one another. They even refer to each other as small islanders and big islanders, which annoys another character, the Governor. In a passionate outburst he reminds them of who they were, and why they were all on the boat, and brings that nonsensical talk to an end. Thus several of the emigrants are forced to reflect and to delve into their past more minutely. They take a long searching look into the future. Whatever happens they hope the future will be different. They are moving towards an uncertainty, but no one wishes to turn back whatever the evidence at the end of the journey. Each has a plan which he hopes will give him that better break. Before the journey ends each has learned more about the other and a little more about the plight of the West Indies.

Mr. Lamming has used the voyage as the occasion for that discovery of Identity. The dialogue which sums this up most cogently, and thus completes the awareness, comes from the Jamaican, and from the Trinidadian, Tornado. In the course of his long speech The Jamaican indulges in some good-humoured vulgarity, but we are brought up sharp with his serious interpretation of West Indian history:

> " ... *history tell me that dese same West Indies people is a sort of vomit you vomit up. Was a long time back England an' France an' Spain an' all the great nations make a raid on whoever live in dem islands. Whatever the book call them me no remember, but most of them get wipe out. Then de great nations make plans for dese islands. England, France, Spain all of them vomit up what them dint want, an' the vomit settle there in that Caribbean Sea. It mix up with the vomit them make Africa vomit, an' the vomit them make India vomit, an' China an' nearly every race under the sun. An' just as vomit never get back in yuh stomach, these people, most of them, never get back where them vomit them from. Them settle right there in the Caribbean Sea, an' de great nations, England an'*

the rest, them went on stirring the mixture , them stir that vomit to suit themselves, an' them stir an' stir till only Gwad knows how, the books ain't tell me yet 'cause my reading' not finish, them stir and stir till the vomit start to take on new life, it was like ammonia, get too strong for them stirring it. Now it exploding bit by bit ... "

In conclusion the Jamaican says that what is happening in the West Indies, what the West Indians are trying to prove, what they are trying to achieve is nothing to be laughed at. His readings into history has revealed to him that people throughout history have been doing the same thing:

"The interpretation me give hist'ry is people the world over always searchin' an' feelin,' from time immemorial , them keep searchin' an' feelin'. Them ain't know w'at is wrong 'cause them ain't know what is right, but them keep searchin' an feelin,'an' when them dead an' gone, history write things 'bout them that them themself would not have know or understand. Them wouldn't know themself if them see themself in his'try. Cause w'at them was tryin' to prove them leave to hist'ry to to give a name."

Tornado is in agreement, and sums up:

"We got to suffer first and then come together, If there is one thing England going to teach all o' we is that there is no place like home no matter how bad home is .....But you got to pay to learn, an' believe me, I may not see it, but those comin' after goin' make better West Indians for comin' up here an' seein' for themself what is what."

What Mr. Lamming is telling us here is that those who had met on the boat and had spoken, belonged not to Jamaica or Barbados or Trinidad, but to the West Indies of the future. Mr. Lamming, the writer and emigrant, is personally involved in the flight along with the others. His involvement is intimate, and his sympathies have been strongly aroused by the suffering he knows and the confusion that that has brought about. His novels spring out of that experience.

Like John Steinbeck's route 66 which the Joads of *The Grapes of*

Wrath had to follow, 'the mother road; the road of flight,' the Atlantic in Mr. Lamming's novel is also the road of flight, and the voyage of the emigrants is meant to make us understand and share a human experience of suffering and resistance.

Out of that history of violence and suffering, that experience of exile, the black West Indian has acquired something of tremendous value – the knowledge of which he must now impart to the other ethnic groups in the Caribbean to whom the question is no less relevant.

Mr. Lamming deals with that in his third novel, *Of Age And Innocence.* The novel is set in the fictional island of San Cristobal, an area with its own unique history and social composition representative of the Caribbean racial admixture. Of the island Mr. Lamming makes the principal personage in the novel, Shepherd, say:

> *"Here Africa and India shook hands with China, and Europe wrinkles like a brow begging every face to promise love. The past is all suspicion, now is an argument that will not end, and to-morrow is like the air in your hand. I know San Cristobal. It is mine, me, divided in harmony that still pursues all its separate parts. No new country, but an old land inhabiting new forms of men who can never resurrect their roots and do not know their nature. Colour is their old and only alphabet. The whites are turning whiter, and the blacks are like an instinct which some voice, my voice shall exercise. San Cristobal so old and yet so new, no place, this land, but a promise. My promise, and perhaps yours too ... "*

That, we can take it, is Mr. Lamming's vision of the promise of the Caribbean.

The novel treats of the traditional imperialistic technique of crushing all revolutionary movements in an attempt to keep the island in subjection. That forms the background of the novel.

Two exiles return from England determined to awake the islanders to political consciousness and to stir them to political activity. Mark, the black writer who has been living in England as an isolated artist, returns home to find his real identity. Shepherd, the other, has been forced back because of his frustration with England and the English woman with whom he had been in love.

While Mark is finding it rather painful in making his adjustment to life on the island, seeking and establishing his identity, Shepherd is perfectly clear in his mind what he wants to do and what he has to do, and he works to accomplish that.

> *"He wanted each group to get an idea of who they were and that must include where they originally came from. When he had planted that in their heads once and for all, what did he do next? He showed them that there was no difference between them, Indian, Negro, Chinese or what you like, in relation to people like me and the Governor and what he calls the fellows at Whitehall. That's what he made clear, and there isn't a soul in San Cristobal, literate or illiterate, young or old, who didn't understand what he was saying. Whatever difference there was between them, they had one thing in common: a colonial past with all that it implies."*

That is how Crabbe, a member of the ruling élite sees what Shepherd is trying to do, and he is perfectly correct in his interpretation.

Shepherd makes that common history, the experience of colonialism, his political platform, and with the commencement of his political activities the people 'talked about the future as though they had discovered a new dimension in time.' Suddenly the people are awakened to the political realities of their situation. They can even share with him his vision of the future, and after one of his passionate speeches, we hear one of his listeners say:

> *"'Tis words make him work his magic," a woman said. "When a man got words he can open my ear."*

> *"An' magic don't take no time to work," said the man "before your eye clap twice you in the spell."*

> *"He move my heart that mornin'" the woman said, "an' if I could have lay my han' on them who say he was mad, only if I could have lay my han' on the lying tongue that try to slander his brain."*

> *"They didn't want him to do the work he start," the man said, "but he choose the right day to make that speech, the mornin' we celebrate San Cristobal. 'Tis a next day o' deliverance he goin' bring.'*

CALIBAN DEMANDS A HEARING   137

> *"An' he ain't talk no lies," the woman said, "he ain't let his tongue slip a single lie when he say San Cristobal is his an' mine, an' how he goin' make it belong to everybody who born here."*
>
> *"'Tis why they say he mad, an' make that disturbance on the plane," said the man, "the spirit must have tell them what plan his mind was makin'."*
>
> *"Those who born here come first," said the woman, "he make it plain as scripture that we got to come first. An' for that they call him mad. But if 'tis mad, 'tis a madness we been waitin' for God only knows how long."*

In an illuminating passage, one of the characters, Paravecino, a member of the Legislative Council, explains to Crabbe, the Chief of Police, what has happened. Shepherd had received his education in England and Crabbe interprets his behaviour back in the island as ungratefulness:

> *"You gave Shepherd an image of yourself, and then circumstances provided him with the opportunity to examine that image. If you had never allowed these colonials to flock to your country as they please, Shepherd might not have happened. So they went, and you know better than I what they found. They found you in a state of disorder which was worse than anything they knew in the colonies. And was their experience of this disorder that suggested to them what could happen when they got back home. In fact they returned home for no other reason. It was you, not the colonials who started the colonial revolution. But you can't have your cake and eat it. You can't pride yourself on liberty and deny them the experiment too. Nor can you go on enjoying the privilege of a lie at the expense of people who have discovered the lie. The image of a superior animal doesn't make sense after these men like Shepherd work in a London factory or sleep whenever he pleases with some little progressive slut from the London School of Economics. You treat men like children and forget that children have a way of growing up. And what they understand is always different from what the parents had imagined."*

One day, by accident, Shepherd encounters Penelope, a white friend of Mark's, along one of the deserted beaches. They had met before on the plane taking Shepherd from London to San Cristobal. From that very first meeting Shepherd had taken a dislike to Penelope. They are both surprised by this present unexpected meeting. They cannot avoid each other, so they talk. The conversation is a long and illuminating one. Penelope had always been curious to discover the reason for Shepherd's hostility towards her. Shepherd confesses the deception of the woman in England with whom he had been in love; Penelope resembles her in every detail, almost. Through her deception, however, he had discovered many things about himself. He had discovered, for example, that until then, until that experience, he tells her:

"I had always lived in the shadow of a meaning which others had placed on my presence in the world, and I had played no part at all in making that meaning, like a chair which is wholly at the mercy of the idea guiding the hand of the man who builds it."

He explains himself and his politics to her. It is not true that it was his experience with the English woman that made him go into politics.

"That experience was only a condition which precipitated my decision. It is truer to say I went into politics in order to redefine myself through action. And just as it was a deception which preceded a certain understanding, it would seem that a certain regression is necessary for any leap I may make, for any other me to emerge."

He brushed a trickle of sweat off his nose and rubbed his hands slowly over the blanket.

"Take the chair again. I begin by behaving like a chair. I am like a chair which understands and revolts by saying, fine I accept that I am a chair, but I shall behave on occasions as though I am not a chair. For example, I will only let you sit on me when I feel like it! Similarly, I accept me as the meaning I speak of has fashioned me. I accept. For all purposes of simple understanding, I agree that I am that me. But from now on, I deny that meaning its authority. When it suits my purpose I shall use it, when it doesn't I shall be hostile. In fact, I am at

> *war. But neither the whites who get scared, nor the natives who are glad quite know my meaning. And they are terrified because I say that if I win power, and there is no doubt about that, I shall begin my business by changing the whole curriculum of privilege in San Cristobal."*

There was a pause, sudden and deliberate. And soon his voice returned, quiet and grave in its new emphasis. He had found some peace in the knowledge which he was about to impart:

> *"And you know something," he continued. "It is not the threat of losing jobs, or living in less extravagant circumstances, which really worry them. They're used to enough personal poverty in Europe. But they are really frightened that the order of privilege which is an essential part of their conception of themselves can be revalued, redistributed, or even abolished completely. They are terrified of becoming like the chair which is defenceless against the idea of chair ... I am the one who now sees them, not they me."*

Shepherd explains further that, contrary to what the whites believe, he is not a cut-throat.

> *"I am just a particular brand of man who, in certain circumstances which are old and may remain with us for a long time, refuses to be that man. When I speak of regression I simply mean that my rebellion begins with an acceptance of the very thing I reject, because my conduct cannot have the meaning I want to give it, if it does not accept and live through that conception by which the others now regard it. What I succeed in doing is changing that conception of me. But I cannot ignore it."*

Penelope understands what he has told her, and she appreciates his determination "To be a man in spite of ... " She burst into tears, and Shepherd wonders 'Was this pity? Or her guilt?' Penelope wants to 'let him know that she understands this feeling which had disfigured his innocence and separated him from himself.' She wants to tell him that he was not alone, but she cannot find the words to convey her meaning. She would like to see him again, perhaps next time 'to let him know that those he called the enemy were equally torn by a similar contradiction which had made him a hero in San Cristobal.'

That section of the novel is the most moving. After the four hundred years of slavery, and then post-emancipation, the author is saying, this is what has emerged: Black and White, Brown and Yellow are all bound up inextricably with one another. Their fulfilment as individuals cannot be separated from the destiny of their people, and that destiny is the same for everyone in the Caribbean. Penelope never gets the chance to see Shepherd again.

The island explodes in sudden violent demonstrations and, whether the islanders wanted it or not, there is bloodshed, for the imperialists have reacted in the only way they know, the only way in which they have been accustomed to react – with bullets and bayonets.

All appears quiet after the violence and the bloodshed, yet the people have not been crushed; they have not been defeated either. Certain of the leaders, including Shepherd, have been killed, that is all. The younger generation knows that it will win in the end; time is on their side. Towards the end of the novel we find three boys, representatives of the island's three racial groups, sitting around the grave of one of the slain, Rowley, discussing the outcome of events, and the future. Some of the arrested are to be tried, and Bob, the Negro, Lee the Chinese, and Sing, the Indian, talk among themselves, the darkness lit by the candles which they had come to place on Rowley's grave:

> " ... *the darkness made fearful strides towards them, and they noticed how the candles wasted away, and the flames collapsed and died. But the earth grew light where they stood. Their gifts still made a quivering fire over Rowley's grave, and they felt that it was he who kept their candles alive, that they would burn forever in a legend which told San Cristobal and the world why they had followed their wish to climb that pitiless cliff which carried the Tribe Boys to their death.*"

"To-morrow is the trial" said Bob.
"To-morrow an' maybe till a next to-morrow it last," Singh said.
"But hardly more," said Bob *"to-morrow an' a next to-morrow."*

Lee did not speak.

The curfew rang, ordering every street to be empty. But they would not stir. They sat in silence beside the grave. And the sound reached them again, irrelevant as the noise of the sea, an ordinary part of the night, like the howl of a dog shut out. The Law could not now enter their feeling.'

Refusing any part of the rivalry that has been tearing their elders apart, the three, Bob, Lee and Singh, represent the spirit of resurrection, that new consciousness, that awareness now of the West Indian identity born of that common heritage of their history of slavery, indentured labour and the experience of colonialism. The creation of that new society is going one step further, one more logical step towards the changing of that order of privilege of which Shepherd had spoken. There is only one condition for its fulfilment: there must be no recrimination.

In an essay entitled *The West Indian People,* Mr. Lamming concludes with the words:

"It is no spirit of arrogance which makes me say that for all their shame and squalor and raggedness of spirit, the inner reality of the West Indian people is unique.

If that uniqueness can ever find its perfect utterance, I believe we shall have created a style of thought and tone of perception, quite natural to ourselves, and truly rewarding to others."

That would be the West Indian contribution, or rather, one of the contributions, to Western civilization.

'O lumière amicale
O fraîche source de la lumière
ceux qui n'ont inventé ni la poudre ni la boussole
ceux qui n'ont jamais dompter la vapeur ni l'électricité
ceux qui n'ont exploré ni les mers ni le ciel
mais ceux sans qui la terre ne serait pas la terre
gibbosité d'autant plus bienfaisante que la terre déserte
davantage la terre
silo ou se préserve et mûrit ce que la terre a de plus terre
ma négritude n'est pas une pierre, sa surdité ruée
contre la clameur du jour
me négritude n'est pas une taie d'eau morte sur
l'oeil mort de la terre
ma négritude n'est ni une tour ni une cathédrale

elle plonge dans la terre rouge du sol
elle plonge dans la chair ardente du ciel
elle troue l'accablement opaque de sa droite patience.'

Aimé Césaire.

O friendly light
o fresh source of light
those who have invented neither the sword nor the compass
those who have tamed neither steam nor electricity
those who have explored neither the ocean nor the heavens
but those without whom the earth would not be the earth
gibbosity all the more beneficient, as the deserted
silo where is preserved and ripened what is
earthiest in earth
my negritude is not a stone, its deafness thrown headlong
against the clamour of the day
my negritude is not a speck of dead water on
the dead eye of the earth
my negritude is neither a tower nor a cathedral

it plunges into the red flesh of the earth
it plunges into the burning flesh of the sky
it bores deep through the opaque dejection of its
upright patience.

CHAPTER 6
The Descent of Black Orpheus

WE BEGAN OUR ANALYSIS OF THE FORCES WHICH WENT into the making of the West Indian people with a look at history, then followed that up with the literature of the West Indian people to discover how they were responding to the challenges of that historical past.

That was done because any sociologist or cultural anthropologist would need to do the same when dealing with the problems of contemporary Caribbean society, and would need constantly to keep that past in view, for at every turn he would be coming across remains of past structures with which he would be dealing.

As Césaire and Franz Fanon have reminded us, however, it is not enough merely to point to that past, for the present is also a function of the past.

What we are examining, therefore, when we look at Caribbean society, is the continuity between the past and the present, the surviving traces which are African, and which are so important to us because they are the basic elements of the contemporary West Indian way of life.

The West Indies to-day is a multi-racial society. All those races and peoples and their admixtures, and the various languages, have made the West Indian a uniquely cosmopolitan man. As Mr. George Lamming has observed. The West Indian has a distinct advantage over all colonized peoples, for unlike other black people in other parts of the world:

"The West Indians, however black and disposed, could never have felt the experience of being in a minority ... This numerical superiority has given the West Indian a certain leisure, a certain experience of relaxation among the white expatriates; for the West Indian has learnt, by sheer habit, to take the white presence for granted."

Césaire was not being at all pedantic when he stated that it is not the West Indian who must try to understand Europe, rather is it Europe which has to understand the West Indian. The question will be asked: How is it, then, that despite that multi racial, multi-ethnic composition of present-day West Indian society, the Hispanic, or the all black as in Haiti, or a percentage of black, a larger percentage of mulatto and an even greater percentage of white, such as in Cuba, or all mulatto as in the Dominican Republic, or the kaleidoscope of colours as in Trinidad and Tobago, Jamaica or Curacao, how is it that the vital expression of Caribbean folk material, the basic ingredient of Caribbean culture, is African?

Why is it so, indeed? Again, as with everything West Indian, it has to do with that unique West Indian historical experience.

In the chapters on History we saw that by the end of the eighteenth century West Indian society was complete. Nothing coming after that was able to alter that society to any marked degree. The people who formed that society were the black slaves, the white slave-owners and plantation owners, and the mulattos, the children of the white men with the black slave women.

The mulattos were, as has been said before, for the most part, house slaves or freed people of colour. They repudiated the African side of their ancestry and chose instead to identify with the Europeans. Because they lived in their fathers' homes they were able to copy European cultural traditions very early. The Europeans never considered the West Indies as their home. The islands were places to come to in order to get rich. But there were some, also, who were sent there as a punishment by their family. Or the West Indies were merely stepping stones to the larger continent, El Dorado, a tendency to which Adam Smith and the Cambridge scholar, Richard Pares, testify. In other words, people were simply passing through, or returning home from the continent of Central and South America.

Even when the band of privateers, buccaneers, filibusters, adventurers, fugitives from justice, escaped galley-slaves, debtors and assorted criminals eventually settled in the islands, real settlement never took place, for example, in the British islands. We can gather that from what they left behind—forts and prisons. That was due primarily to the transient nature, also, the absentee nature of the British occupation of the islands. Nothing else that could be considered of any value as in the construction of cities as the Spaniards did. They did not even erect schools for their own people but sent their children to be educated in Europe.

What we are witnessing during those three hundred years of

Caribbean history is the stress on England and France as home for the white influential people and an attitude towards the islands which in turn led to the stress on education outside the West Indies rather than building suitable schools for the area. Home was always somewhere else, so that we find that the people who owned everything, who, if they had settled in the islands would have been the people to have established any influence there were absent. They made their contributions elsewhere — Europe.

What did that mean, in terms of what was to follow, that is, the effect of that kind of attitude upon the people who had chosen to identify with the Europeans, the mulattos who lived in the homes of their fathers? Inevitably, they, also, turned their gaze towards Europe, the Mother Country. Becky Sharp, the wealthy mulatto woman in Thackeray's *Vanity Fair,* went to Europe to be educated. In language, dress, marriage customs, religion, total culture, in fact, they became Europe oriented.

When Sir Vidia Naipaul says that nothing of value was created in the West Indies, he is perfectly correct, but only in so far as concerns the Europeans and the Mulattos. But, not so with the Blacks.

The Blacks who were taken to the West Indies brought their culture with them, for a people, wherever they go, do not leave themselves behind. They do not discard that culture as though it were an old shirt, or dirty underwear which can be taken off at leisure.

For several centuries these black slaves lived in the rural areas, having little or no contact with the Europeans, and so remained cut off and unaffected by white cultural influences to any large extent. Thus they were able to hold on to their African-ness and things African — their songs, musical traditions, dances, folk tales, their knowledge of herbal medicines where they found similar herbs in the islands, above all, their African religions which they were able to practice in secret.

What we are concerned with here is the question of African survivals in the Caribbean, those things which have been handed down and are African in origin, and which are social and cultural.

We shall use the adjective African in its widest sense here, for Africa is a vast continent containing a multitude of nations and a diversity of cultural traditions. In the Caribbean of the slave society all those differences were ignored in the process of moulding the plantation slaves. So also was the social development of the islands. As we have seen before, each island had established its own particular association with its particular metropolitan country and its own religions, linguistic and cultural affiliations. It has been possible, in certain instances, to specify to which nation certain inherited cultural traits belong. For example, Voodoo in Haiti and Cuba came from Dahomey, Guinea and the Congo. Shango in Cuba and Trinidad from the Yoruba in Nigeria.

There are, however, a set of cultural traditions which the peoples of the different African nations have in common. Some interesting work has been done in exploring and isolating those differences and commonalities by certain cultural anthropologists, for example, Roger Bastide *African Civilizations in the New World*, Melville J. Herskovits, *The Myth of the Negro Past*, Trinidad and Tobago's Dr. J.D. Elder *The Yoruba Ancestral Cult In Gasparillo*, William Bascom *Shango in the New World*.

In isolating the differences and at the same time identifying some of the common features, we must also bear in mind the intervention of the various European powers and the imposition by those Europeans of various social and cultural traits. Again a number of the islands changed hands several times that to-day we can regard them as cosmopolitan in their cultural influences.

Yet, all that does not obscure the West African base line which dominates throughout the entire Caribbean.

We gather from Moreau de St. Mery, Pierre Francois de Charlevoix, Richard Ligon, and others who had been on the spot at the time that the slaves came from various parts of Africa. They came, also, from a variety of nations — Yolofs, Foules, Sosos, Bambaras, Bouriques, Mesurades, Aradas, Caplous, Fonds, Mais, Fantins, Mayombes, Mousombes, and many others as listed by Moureau de St. Mery, the most observant of the chroniclers; he even details the characteristics of the these various African peoples.

Those people also came from all walks of life. On the plantations they were all reduced to one thing, to one common purpose. They were thrown together, people of different backgrounds, different languages, different religious beliefs, different traditions. Each brought something of his past and poured it into the new amalgam which was to be that unique historical and social category of being — the West Indian.

Those various peoples were also exposed, as mentioned earlier, and subjected constantly to ways and ideas which were altogether foreign to them. Inevitably, in the course of time, they absorbed some of those ideas and worked out something new, something distinctly their own out of those many different and often contradictory European elements. Yet they managed to retain elements of their African social and cultural heritage which had proved of such immense spiritual and psychological advantage to them.

That is what makes the Caribbean such an interesting area of study for social and cultural anthropologists. How much was retained and how much lost? Of what remains, how much has been changed, and to what extent?

Some investigators have discovered that it is only those islands that were French or Spanish, or for long periods had been under French domination, that African cultural traditions are maintained, for example, and has been mentioned earlier, Yoruba culture in Cuba and Trinidad and Tobago, Dahomey, Guinea and the Congo in Haiti.

The French and the Spaniards are Catholics and the Catholic church regarded the slaves as souls to be saved. As far as the Catholics were concerned, the slaves were complete human beings and that the only difference between the slaves and their owners were worldly and transient things. The Catholic church, apparently, did not obliterate everything African from the minds of the slaves. So we find in those islands and territories the people could afford to be good Christians and at the same time practice their various African religions, in certain instances even identifying similarities in the Christian and African deities. Maya Deren in her book *The Divine Horsemen*, has shown how that has worked.

In several particulars African and Christian religious myths and rituals show similarities, the beginning of the world, for example, the creation of the first man and woman, the idea of the Soul, the existence of the Supreme Being and the emphasis on the power of the word which represents the life force in both African and Christian religious beliefs. It is through the power of the word that all life is produced.

The Christian god said: "Let there be light!" and there was light. The African, placing the same emphasis on the power of the word, says:

"I shall say trees
I shall say storm
I shall say fire ... "

And those things appear, the word being the creative force which causes things and maintains them. The word is an incantation as with the Christians, and what it produces it names.

Many of the missionaries who went to Africa to spread the word after the abolition of slavery and the slave trade, inevitably came into conflict with the Africans, considering them to be heathens and savages, incapable even of conceiving of anything approaching the existence of a God. It came as a surprise to many of those missionaries when the Africans vigorously defended their beliefs and showed that those beliefs were rational. Dr. E. Bolaji Idowu, in his book *Olodumare—God In Yoruba Belief*, provides us with an excellent study of religion in West Africa in his interpretation of the Yoruba concept of the Supreme Deity, Olodumare. There are other works, also, which throw light on African religious beliefs some of which show parallels with other cultures such as the Egyptian and the Judaic-Christian. Jean-Pierre Hallet's study of the African pygmies, for example, *Pygmy Kitabu*, Father Placid Tempel's *La Philosophie Bantu*, or Marcel Griaule's *Conversations With Ogotemmeli* a fascinating book about the religious ideas of the Dogon people of the Sudan.

In a novel by Mongo Beti of the Cameroons, entitled *Le Pauvre Christ de Bomba*, a missionary who upon his arrival had managed to get large numbers of Africans to attend his church, wondered why, upon his return after a short absence, the Africans no longer came to the church. His catechist gives one explanation which does not entirely please the cook, a young African named Zachari. Zachari tells the missionary:

> *"The first of us who ran to religion, your religion, came to it as a sort of ... revelation. Yes, that's it, a revelation; a school where they could learn your secret, the secret of your power, or your aeroplanes and railways ... in a word, the secret of your mysteries. Instead of that, you began talking to them about God, of the Soul, of eternal life, and so forth. Do you really suppose they didn't know those things already long before you came?"*

The African, then, had a Soul, a conception of God long before the arrival of the Europeans. Not one god but several gods, like the ancient Europeans themselves. Whatever happened to those African gods? Mr. Derek Walcott tells us:

> " ... *We left*
> *somewhere a life we never found,*
> *customs and gods that are not born again,*
> *some crib, some grill of light*
> *clanged shut on us in darkness, and withheld*
> *us from that world below us and beyond,*
> *and in its swaddling cerements we're still bound.*"

That was not entirely correct. Not all the customs and gods had been left behind. Despite the Middle Passage, or perhaps because of it, those who survived had to hold on to their beliefs; otherwise the Europeans would have succeeded in exterminating yet another race of people. Such was the tenacity, however, of the Africans who had been torn from their roots and had been taken to the Caribbean, that though mutilated, they took root in the new soil and grew strong again, as Guy Tirolien had shown in his poem *Afrique*.

The torn branch from that African tree, transplanted in the Caribbean, had survived in that alien soil, its roots had plunged deep, very deep into those waters below and beyond that island below the sea, Africa. In the process there had to be some adjustments, inevitably, a re-interpretation of the functions of some of the African gods, for example, and in some instances, the invention of new deities, like Petro. That needs some explanation.

African societies, judging by the dramatization in the novels which treat of traditional village life, were well stabilized hierarchical societies; very religious, with the different deities playing their roles of protecting the people from whatever might threaten them. Those gods were not vengeful gods, and in all other respects had many identifiable human attributes. They could be consulted, cajoled, even bribed. They had their favourite foods and drinks, and would even sulk if they were neglected for any length of time. The gods of ancient Greece manifested those same characteristics as well.

In the Caribbean the Blacks found to their horror after that traumatic experience of the Middle Passage, that conditions in their new environment were vastly more different, even hostile, than they ever could have imagined. All the things that they had evolved for themselves in Africa were disrupted, broken and brutally violated. They discovered to their utmost horror and despair that the traditional attitudes of their African deities could not cope; they needed new deities to deal with that hostile and uniquely horrifying situation in which they now found themselves. Aggression, anger, vengeance, violence were what were needed. Hence Petro, a more practical deity, unforgiving, one of action and vengefulness, violent, was born. The ceremony for him is more emotional, the dancing is more tense, and the drumming, even, reveals a nervousness, and a raging tension that had been absent in traditional Africa where the deities had never prepared them for the injustices which they were now suffering in the Caribbean slave society.

Some cultural anthropologists who are familiar with West African societies maintain that the slaves, in particular runaway slaves who had been converted by the Amerindians with whom they had come into contact in the jungles, and with whom they had joined forces, found it necessary to create a god of vengeance, one which would need blood and sacrifices. Such were the gods of the Amerindians, and the Africans had never been averse to borrowing or copying those deities from other peoples with whom they came into contact, once those deities could be useful to them.

That is why they were able to couple their African or Caribbean derived deities with the Catholic Saints which they had discovered shared similar characteristics. Indeed, that is also one of the answers to the question of how it was possible to have only two West African religions dominant in the Caribbean, considering the multitude of nations with their different beliefs. The slaves looked for deities with special functions, and where one nation dominated, or rather the people of one nation dominated, the others followed their pattern of worship.

Above all, as Herskovits and other cultural anthropologists have revealed in their examination and study of both West African and Caribbean societies, there were a number of similarities amongst the peoples of the African nations to enable them to form the basis for a retention of African beliefs and customs despite the crushing horrors, disruption and chaos of slavery on the plantations. For instance, the peoples of those different nations worshipped different gods, but in their religious worship magic played an important part. Herskovits informs us that magic constitutes only one aspect of religious systems to be found in West Africa. The ancestral cult is another aspect of West African beliefs, with the spirits of the dead envisaged as living in another world, yet alert to manifest power among their descendants.

Indeed, several of those aspects of West African beliefs and customs were later to constitute the themes of some of the finest poetry. About the dead, for example, the Senegalese poet, David Diop, says:

> *"Those who are dead are never dead.*
> *They are in the thickening shadows,*
> *The dead are not under the earth.*
> *They are in the tree that rustles,*
> *They are in the wood that groans,*
> *They are in the water that runs,*
> *They are in the water that sleeps,*
> *They are in the hut, they are in the crowd,*
> *The dead are never dead."*

Mr. George Lamming describes a religious ceremony in Haiti known as the ceremony of the Souls at which is heard at first hand, the secrets of the dead. My Lamming tells us:

> *"The celebrants are mainly relatives of the deceased who ever since death have been locked in water. It is the duty of the dead to return and offer, on this momentous night, a full and honest report of their past relations with the living. A wife may have to say why she refused love to her husband; a husband may have to say why he deprived his wife of their children's affections. It is the duty of the Dead to speak, since their release from the Purgatory of Water cannot be realized until they have fulfilled the contract which the ceremony symbolizes. The Dead need to speak if they are to enter that eternity which will be their last and permanent Futures. The living demand to hear whether there is any need for forgiveness, for redemption; whether, in fact, there may be any guide which may help them towards reforming their present condition. Different as they may be in their present state of existence, those alive and those now Dead ... their ambitions point to a similar end. They are interested in their Future.*
>
> *Through the medium of the Priest, the Dead speak of matters which it must have been difficult to raise before; and through the same medium the living learn and understand what the Dead tongues have uttered."*

What Mr. Laming is emphasizing is the close relationship that exists between the Dead and the Living.

To continue, then, with the similarities. In ceremonials we find that in all the West African religions there is the worship of the gods through the dance. We also find the phenomenon of possession by the deities, the state when, for the period of that possession, the devotees assume all the characteristics of the particular deity. (No two deities can possess the same person at one and the same time). The music, that is the drums and other percussion instruments which form the special character of these various religious ceremonies.

The various West African religions had all those elements in common, and in the Caribbean of the slave society all the slaves, irrespective of their tribal affiliations, practiced them. As has been said earlier, where the people of one nation were numerically dominant, their system of beliefs was adopted, and prevailed. In Haiti, as has been pointed out before, the majority of the slaves came from Dahomey, followed by those from Guinea and the Congo. Thus we have Voodoo. In Cuba, Trinidad and Grenada, the Yoruba people brought with them the Shango religion.

The Shango religion requires no formal initiation ceremony as with Voodoo, but simply the ceremonial washing of the head to dedicate it to the deity, for when possession takes place, the god takes control of the devotee by entering the individual's head.

Voodoo, the most popular and the most misunderstood, like most religions, adheres to certain basic premises. The African has a soul and believes in a Supreme Being. The Voodoo adherents have conceived of Man as possessing a material body animated by a spirit that is Man's soul which, unlike the material body, being non-material, does not die when the body dies. This soul may achieve the status of a divinity, a lao, to use the Voodoo terminology, which, to the Voodoo adherents becomes the archetypal representative of some natural or moral principle.

In Western Christian societies monuments are built in honour of a man or woman who has done great deeds for his or her country, or who stood for certain laudable principles, so that the memory and achievements of that individual, the principle for which that person stood, may be kept alive. Thus a Chaucer, a Shakespeare, a Milton, a Wellington, a Nelson, a Churchill, or the spirit of Dunkirk in 1940, will be immortalized in stone or in steel. In Christianity, that person will be made a saint. In Voodoo such an individual, or principle, or spirit, is made a lao, a divinity which is ever present and which can be consulted at any time. Thus all the precious accumulation of that individual's intelligence, experience and history are preserved forever, and can be utilized by those of the living who require them.

Voodoo, therefore, is a genuine religion, but unlike Christianity with which it shares certain characteristics, and, unlike Christianity where one can be a good Christian and yet not adhere to any Christian practices, or where one may go to church and pretend to be a Christian and yet not believe in the tenets of the teachings of Christianity, it is not so with Voodoo. One either believes, or one does not. If one believes, then one practices, for belief and practice are synonymous.

Melville J. Herskovits, Harold Courlander and Maya Deren are correct when they say that Voodoo is an integrated system of concepts concerning human behaviour, the relation of mankind to those who have lived before, and to the natural and supernatural forces of the Universe. That is what any genuine religion tries to explain. Voodoo also relates the relationship of the living to those yet unborn. It makes meaningful all apparently unexplained events by showing them to be consistent with established principles in its attempt to tie the unknown to the known and thereby create order out of what had seemed to be pure chaos. As the philosopher, Spinoza, had tried to show, there are no accidents in the Universe. Everything can be explained and made meaningful.

Voodoo went one further than the Christian religion in the matter of the spiritual explanations demanded for the numberless daily occurrences which appeared to puzzle the worshippers. A god who ruled over this immense Universe would be too busy a deity to clutter his mind with the multitude of tiny details about his subjects. So, like the ancient Greeks and Romans, and like their ancestors in Africa with their numerous personal gods or chi, there were created in the Caribbean slave society a hierarchy of gods and goddesses, less powerful than the Omnipotent. Thus if a man's crop failed, or an illness occurred in seemingly inexplicable circumstances, that man would appeal to the particular lao for help. Whatever the problems or dilemmas, and however personal, these were looked after by the particular lao in charge of such things.

Lord Macaulay in his *Lays of Ancient Rome*, begins the poem entitled *Horatio* with an invocation to the nine Roman gods:

*"Lars Porsena of Clusium
By the nine gods he swore
That the great house of Tarquin
Shall suffer wrongs no more.
By the nine gods he swore it ... "*

In the Catholic religion those nine gods have been replaced by the Angels and Saints. A Catholic seldom prays directly to the Almighty, but very often asks the Virgin Mary, the Mother of God, or one of the Saints, to intercede on his behalf.

The ancient Geeks did the same. In Homer's *Iliad*, for example, when it was decreed by Zeus that one of the heroes was to die, the hero's mother, who was herself one of the minor deities, went to plead with Zeus, the father of all the gods, to spare her son's life. Her argument was emotionally understandable. Why must it be her son who must die? she wanted to know. Using her feminine charms she demanded reassurances of Zeus's affection for her, and pleaded further "Promise me this thing verily, and bow thy head thereto, that I may know full well how I, among gods, am least in honour."

We cannot have anything more human than that. To put her request into more modern, Hollywood-type romantic fashion : "If you do not grant me this favour, then you do not love me. It's some other woman whom you love .So my son, and not the other woman's son who is to die. How cruel can you be, Zeus!"

Or perhaps she had imagined that she had upset Zeus in some way, and the death of her son was the punishment which she had to pay.

So it is with Voodoo. It does not conceive of life as a struggle between good and evil, but that since human beings can generally be persuaded into any mood, so can the gods. For, after all, they were created by humans. And as there is variety in human personality, so likewise are the gods not immutable or infallible.

That is where Voodoo and Christianity part company in the similarities and go their separate ways, for a white person who is a Christian and who attempts to reconcile an all-loving Father with all the evils that He allows, perhaps even condones, in this world would almost certainly end up a neurotic. Not so with Voodoo. Its adherents, by conceiving the spirits, the laos, in manner and desires resembling themselves can understand the Universe without subjecting themselves to that bewilderment which faces the simple

European Christians; a bewilderment which, in the final analysis, forces them to reject their churches, turning them, as this writer has seen in London, into warehouses, shops or youth clubs, and lately, into Mosques.

Sometimes Africa in the Caribbean is not altogether dominant. but forms one of the base lines of whatever the Blacks in the Caribbean have worked out for themselves out of the diverse elements to which they were subjected. That is so, for instances, in several of the dances. One in particular is the Calypso. Not only in the dance, but in the Christian religions which have been introduced into the lives of the Blacks, we find the African element playing a very definite role. The Rastafarian cult is the best known in that respect. Implicit in their philosophy is their commitment to Africa and their rejection of European and North American values.

Decades after the Rastafarians had been advocating their doctrine of self-realization and self-respect for the black man, black people the world over began to embrace those doctrines in their need and their desires to re-define themselves.

That re-definition is now taking serious and even provocative shape in the new cultural expressions emerging in the Caribbean. We see that in the works of poets such as Derek Walcott, Edward Brathwaite, Aimé Césaire, Denis Scott, Nicolas Guillen, and in the novels of Wilson Harris, George lamming, Jacques Roumain, Joseph Zobel, Garth St. Omer, and others. We see it, also, in the works of the historian Elsa Goveia, Dr. Eric Williams and C.L.R. James.

Mr. George Lamming has always pointed out in his novels, in particular, *Season Of Adventure,* that it is the artist who must and has been pointing the way now that colonialism has come to an end and the time of reconstruction is upon the people of the Caribbean. The Caribbean artist to-day is indeed speaking through several media—the Dance, the Steel Band, Drama, Poetry, the Novel, the Plays, Reggae, the Calypso, and, above all, the cricket of Sir Garfield Sobers and Brian Lara and all the other cricketers who have so masterfully distinguished themselves in the game.

All those people, artists in their own right, are working towards an alternative to the European and North American cultural traditions which had been imposed upon them and which, as Mr. C. L. R. James has pointed out in *Beyond A Boundary,* they had more or less accepted and absorbed. Said Mr. James:

> *"It was only years after that I understood the limitation on spirit, vision and self-respect which was imposed on us by the fact that our masters, our curriculum, our code of morals, everything, began from the basis that Britain was the source of all light and learning, and our business was to admire, wonder, imitate, learn; our criterion of success was to have succeeded in approaching that distant ideal...to attain it was, of course, impossible. Both masters and boys accepted it as in the very nature of things. The masters could not be offensive about it because they thought it was their function to do this, if they thought about it at all; and, as for me, it was the beacon that beckoned me on."*

To-day the West Indian people are looking at their own folk cultural tradition as an alternative. When the Haitians rebelled at the end of the eighteenth century, that was precisely what they, also, had announced ... their rejection of the Judaic-Christian theology and philosophy and they replaced those with the worship of the laos, that hierarchy of Voodoo gods and goddesses which were their own and which they had brought with them from Africa. They showed above all that their own, of which they were proud, was as potent or perhaps even more so, culturally, than the European impositions.

What the Haitians had set in motion the rest of the Caribbean people have taken up, in that they preferred to create their own values, rejecting advice and guidance from outside. Such a decision allows them to be free to experiment with whatever elements are at hand. Above all it allows them to be able to move towards that meeting point which will enable them to produce art forms that are closer to the West Indian people and to express that unique historical and social experience of the West Indian people.

Edward Brathwaite has expressed that feeling, that groping towards the alternative, most beautifully in one of his poems when he says:

> *I*
> *must be give words to shape my name*
> *to the syllable of trees.*
>
> *I*
> *must be given words to fashion futures*
> *Like a healer's hand.*

THE DESCENT OF BLACK ORPHEUS

I
must be given words so that the
bees
in my blood's buzzing brain of memory
will make flowers, will make flocks of birds,
will make sky, will make heaven,
the heaven open to the thunder-stone and the
volcano
and the unfolding land.

"Et nous sommes debout maintenant, mon pays et moi, les cheveux
dans le vent, ma main petite maintenant dans son poing énorme et
la force n'est pas en nous, mais au-dessus de nous, dans un voix
qui vrille la nuit et l'audience comme la pénétrance d'une guêpe
apocalyptique. Et la voix prononce que l'Europe nous a pendant
des siècles gavés de mensonges et gonflés de pestilences,
car il n'est point vrai que l'oeuvre de l'homme est finie
que nous n'avons rien à faire au monde
qui nous parasitons le monde
qu'il suffit que nous nous mettions au pas du monde
mais l'oeuvre de l'homme vient seulement de commencer
et il reste à l'homme à conquérir toute interdiction immobilisée
aux coins de sa ferveur
et aucune race ne possède le monopole de la beauté, de l'intelligence,
de la force
et il est place pour tous au rendez-vous de la conquête ... "

Aimé Césaire.

"And we are standing now, my country and I,
hair in the wind, my little hand now in its enormous fist and
force is not in us, but above us, in a voice
which pierces the night and the audience like the sting of an of an
apocalyptic hornet.
and the voice declares that for centuries Europe has stuffed us with
lies and bloated us with pestilence,
for it is not true that the work of man is finished
that we have nothing to do in the world
that we are parasites in the world
that it is enough for us to keep in step with the world
but the work of man is only now beginning
and it remains for man to conquer all the interdictions locked up
in the recesses of his passion
and no race possesses a monopoly of beauty, of intelligence,
of force
and there is a place for all of us at the rendezvous of victory ... "

CHAPTER 7
The Final Pattern

IN HIS BOOK OF ESSAYS AND REFLECTIONS IN EXILE, *The Pleasures of Exile,* Mr. George Lamming gave an explanation of how it became possible for all those different peoples and races to be living together in the Caribbean relatively free of racial conflicts of the sort that has beset the United States of America and had existed in South Africa under Apartheid. Mr. Lamming writes:

> *"The world met here and it was at every level except administration, a peasant world. In one way or another, these people, forced to use a common language which they did not possess on arrival, have had to make something of their surroundings ... "*

One of Trinidad's leading calypsonians, The Mighty Sparrow, no great intellectual like George Lamming, but a West Indian in every sense of the word, has put it in the manner and form which every West Indian, literate or illiterate, can learn and understand; he has composed a Calypso about the racial admixture.

What Sparrow points out in that Calypso in relation to the different ethnic groups in the Caribbean, and in particular, Trinidad and Tobago, is that Indians in India do not play Steel Band, Chinese do not play it either in China, neither do the Europeans in their respective countries. Indians in India do not sing Calypsos, neither do the Chinese in China, nor the Europeans in Europe. Sparrow continues down the West Indian ethnic and cultural line listing those things which were not indigenous to those countries whence had come those people now living in the Caribbean, and who now are West Indians.

What we are talking about here is the creolization of all those peoples and races, all of whom were immigrants imported into the Caribbean, or had been induced to come there for specific reasons. Once there they had to make something of their lives as a matter of survival. It was not a matter of one fighting the other. They soon discovered that they had a common enemy — Europe and European

capitalism in an exploitative colonial setting. They had been taken to the Caribbean for a specific purpose: producing goods for export to the metropolitan countries.

When, for example, we discover that for a time both black slaves and white indentured labourers had worked side by side, both being subjected to injustices, we begin to understand why racial conflict is not endemic to the area. The common enemy was Injustice, against which West Indians of every race and colour have been such fierce fighters. We must be quite clear about that, otherwise we shall never get to understand the West Indian people.

The Martiniquan poet/politician, Aimé Césaire, had made the West Indian attitude to Injustice very plain where he wrote:

> *"You know, however, my tyrannical love,*
> *you know that it is not out of hatred for*
> *other races*
> *that I have chosen to labour for this unique race*
> *that what I want is for universal hunger,*
> *universal thirst ... "*

Some years ago a black South African novelist, Peter Abrahams, decided to make his home in the Caribbean and settled in Jamaica. In a novel which, so far, has been the first by an African on the West Indies and about West Indians, *This Island Now*, he observed that the West Indians are a remarkable people, and gave it as his opinion that the West Indians are far more advanced than those people in several other parts of the world in the matter of race relations, an absence of which in any overt form, he had noticed.

It was the West Indians experience of slavery, indentured labour and colonialism that had made that possible, as Mr. Lamming and Sparrow had indicated. As for slavery, the very nature of plantation life made inevitable the racial admixture which has become a marked feature of Caribbean society. Consider this, for example: the owner of a slave woman took her as his lover, or his mistress, as was the custom and the pattern that had been established throughout the Caribbean. They have children. Neither the law nor the churches, nor social ostracism had succeeded in preventing that. So the family of a slave owner flowed over into the slave quarters and thus began the social integration that was to have no end to this day. That which has been so volatile in other parts of the world, has virtually disappeared in the Caribbean. To have attempted even to have raised it, or to have made it permanent in the Caribbean would have been meaningless, anyway.

When, therefore, at the end of the nineteenth and the beginning of the twentieth centuries the three other racial groups — Indians, Chinese and East Indians — arrived in the Caribbean as indentured labourers, they came into a society that had already been formed, and that society was one which, more or less, had been stabilized. Some did try to maintain their own cultural forms, but the Caribbean being what it is, those new arrivals had been forced to conform, that is, to become creolized.

What, then, do we mean by Creole and creolization?

In the Caribbean, the accepted definition is a people born in, native to, and committed to living in the Caribbean area as from the eighteenth century onwards.

The indigenous peoples — Caribs and Arawaks — had disappeared from the region by that time, so that the process of acculturation and inter-culturation which began in the Caribbean took place first between Black and White, that is, between Europe and Africa, and in an environment that was completely new to both ethnic groups. Both had to make the adjustment to that new environment, and to one another. The atmosphere was one of a Master and Slave relationship in the beginning. Then later came emancipation and colonialism, and another new form of relationship was established.

The word, Creole, first appeared in Cuba. The Barbadian historian and poet, Edward Brathwaite, gives us his definition of Creole and states that:

> "The term creolization, then, is a specialized version of the two widely accepted terms acculturation and inter-culturation : the former referring to the process of absorption of one culture by another, the latter to a more reciprocal activity, a process of inter-mixture and enrichment, each to each."

It further supposes, Mr. Brathwaite continues:

> "a situation where the society concerned is caught up in some kind of colonial arrangement with a metropolitan power, on the one hand, and a plantation arrangement on the other, and where the society is multi-racial but organized for the benefit of a minority of European origin."

What Mr. Brathwaite is suggesting here is that the society which emerged out of that experience is a rather complex one involving a reaction to external metropolitan pressures, and at the same time to internal adjustments made necessary by the juxtaposition of master and labour, White and non-White, Europe and colony, European and African, 'in a culturally heterogeneous relationship.'

What the Caribs have left behind and which forms some elements of Caribbean life are some names of places (Jamaica and Haiti have retained their original Carib names), the Carib prow, now rarely seen for they are being replaced by the fibreglass boats from overseas, the cassava manioc, certain foods and poisonous plants, the tradition of clay pot making, basket weaving

In French Guyana there are four Amerindian tribes — Arawak, the Galibi, the Emerillons and the Wayanas. The Emerillons and the Wayanas keep very much to themselves and do not participate in the social and cultural life of the country.

Each tribe is organized according to its own ancestral customs in its separate villages. Their dwellings are huts built invariably along the riverbanks and those huts are raised on stilts and covered with palm fronds. Their sleeping accommodations are hammocks which in the early years of Negro habitation in the Caribbean islands, before the arrival of motor vehicles and ambulances were copied by the ex-slaves and used for transporting the sick to hospital.

Antonio Benitez-Rojo says in his book, *The Repeating Island* that 'Creole culture's most important signs were found in popular music and dance 'which emerged towards the end of the sixteenth century, out of the interplay of European and African components.' In addition to those components is to be added that of the cuisine—Creole cooking which Ligon describes in his book *A True And Exact History of the Barbados*, and which seems to have attracted many visitors of the Caribbean society even to this day. There are several accounts and descriptions of the various local vegetables, fruits, meats, poultry and fishes and rum and juices that were served in those days by visitors and residents alike. For example, Ligon describes the recipe for the making of Mauby, a specialized Barbadian drink, the recipe for which is completely different from what we know to-day. That drink, Ligon tell us, after having described the various drinks made on the island, that:

> *"The first, and that is used most on the Island, is Mobie, a drink made of Potatoes, and thus done. Put the Potatoes into a tub of water, and, with a broom, stir them up and down; till they are washed clean; then take them out, and put them into a large iron or brass pot, such as you boyl beef in, in England; and put to them as much water, as will only cover a quarter part of them; and cover the top of the pot with a piece of thick canvas doubled, or such cloth as sacks are made with, covering it close, that the steam go not out. Then make a little fire underneath, so much only as will cause the roots to stew; and when they are soft, take them out, and with your hands, squeeze, break, and mash them very small, in fair water; letting them stay there, till the water has drawn and suckt out all the spirit of the roots; which will be done in an hour or two. Then put the liquor and roots into a large woolen bag, like a jelly-bag, pointed at the bottom; and let it run through that, into a jar, and within two hours it will begin to work. Cover it, and let it stand till the next day, and then 'tis fit to be drunk."*

Ligon tells us further that 'There are two several layers, in which the roots grow; one makes the skins of the Potatoes white, the other red: And where the red roots grow, the Mobie, will be red like Claret wine; the other white.' He also describes the several other kinds of drinks made in the island, such as Perino, a drink made by the Amerindians from the roots of the 'Casssvy' (cassava manioc), Grippo, about which he knows nothing of how it is made, Punch made of 'water and sugar put together, which in ten dayes standing will be very strong, and fit for labourers.' Another is the Plumb-drink, 'made of wild Plumbs, which grow here in great abundance, upon very large trees, which being press'd, and strayned, give a very sharp, and poynant flaver ... '

Then there is the Plantine-drink. 'But the drink of the Plantine, is far beyond all these; gathering them full ripe, and the height of their sweetness, we pill them off the skin, and mash them in water well boyl'd; and after we have let them stay there a night, we strain it, and bottle it up, and in a week drink it; and it is very strong and pleasant drink, but it is to be drunk but sparingly, for it is much stronger than Sack, and is apt to mount up into the head.'

Another drink is what Ligon calls the 'Beveridge,' which is made of white sugar, spring water 'and the juyce of Oranges. Then there was the 'Wine of Pines' which we must take to mean the Pineapple which he says is the best kind of drink in the world 'And is certainly the Nectar which the Gods drunk; for on earth there is none like it; and is made of the pure juyce of the fruit it self, without commixture of water, or any other creature, having in it self, a natural compound of all tastes excellent, that the world can yield. This drink is too pure to keep long; in three or four dayes it will be fine; 'tis made by pressing the fruit and straining the liquor, and it is kept in bottles.'

Ligon then also describes the different kinds of meat to be had on the island, and they were, indeed, plentiful.

From that we can gather that the Planters, and their visitors, lived well in the islands, although he was describing Barbados in the seventeenth century.

Several cultural anthropologist have pointed out that the Negro slaves, and later ex-slaves, contributed greatly to the formation of Creole culture, the cuisine above mentioned being one of the components. Next to Haiti, Cuban culture shows the most African influence in the Caribbean, and that influence is reflected and manifested in religious beliefs, music, dance, painting, folklore and literature.

Many artists in Cuba — Fernando Ortiz, the ethno-musicologist, José Marti, the journalist, Nicolas Guillen, the poet, Alejo Carpentier, the novelist, Wilfredo Lam, the painter, are some of them — recognized the cultural possibilities in the Afro-Cuban influence. José Marti, for example, in much of his political writings, proposed the idea, not only in Cuba, but all of Latin America, of a mestizo or mixed race continent — Creole, the people: Black, White and mulatto who were born in the Caribbean from the eighteenth century onwards.

By 1820, says David Lowenthal, more than two-thirds of the Negroes in the Caribbean were Creole. Creole, he says, is a condition, rather than a nationality. In Martinique and Guadeloupe, the current movement and debate is centred around the question: 'Créolité; or; 'Antillanité?' From that we can gather than the Blacks in the French Antilles are still grappling with the question of Identity — 'Qui et quels nous sommes?' But we shall return to that later.

The word, as was said earlier, is of Spanish origin, and denotes people born in the Caribbean, but, again, according to Lowenthal, has been extended to include songs, habits, things, customs, ideas, and cuisine. The word, though, has been given different meanings in different islands and even on the mainland territories of the Guyanas and in Brazil as well. There are also different types of Creole—English, Spanish, Dutch Creole, as well as the French Creole spoken in the islands and territories which were once French colonies—Haiti, Guadeloupe, Dominica, Martinique, Saint Lucia, certain parts of Grenada and Trinidad, French Guyana, The Seychelles, Mauritius and Union in the Indian Ocean. Also spoken in New Orleans and Louisiana in the Southern United States of America.

Again, according to the Barbadian historian and poet, Edward Brathwaite, the word Creole, in Peru refers to people of Spanish descent born in the New World. In Brazil, on the other hand, it applies to Negro slaves born locally. While in Sierra Leone, it refers to the descendants of former slaves and poor Blacks from Britain who settled along the coast and who form a social élite distinct from the native Africans.

In Jamaica, the word Creole was used to denote Blacks, Whites and Mulattos who were born in and committed to the area. That is now the accepted definition of the word in the Caribbean.

Creolization, then, is a way of life very different from that of the white metropolitan countries, and those who arrived in the West Indies — Blacks and Whites and who came from different cultural backgrounds, their adjustment to the new environment, and their interaction with each other; what emerged which was different from what they had known, had practiced at home, and had to change in response to the circumstances in which they found themselves. In short, the social process which took place and which came to be known as Creolization, and the new society — Creole Society.

To conform to the life and values which they had known at home was impossible in the Caribbean and all were soon caught up in that new process, that new system and style of living in which moral standards and values were non-existent. Some irresistible force seemed to have drawn them and compelled them into that new life, made them, in fact, as Brathwaite says, 'perform in certain roles which, in fact, they quickly came to believe in.' The process of Creolization had begun.

Socialization among the slaves working together in groups, and communal participation in social and recreational activities— drumming, singing and dancing — also worked towards Creolization.

As has been shown before, there were also different groups who were closest to the Europeans — House slaves, domestics, female slaves who were the lovers and concubines of the white men. Those soon began to imitate the Whites' lifestyle, mode of dress, and language. There were other practices which also worked towards Creolization as Lady Nugent has noted in her Journal.

As has been noted above, even in the matter concerning food, the Whites had become creolized. Bryan Edwards, a planter and slave-owner, tells how he disdained European or English dishes and prefers Creole dishes, such as 'plantains, bananas, yams of several varieties, calalue (a species of spinnage), eddoes, cassava, and sweet potatoes. A mixture of these, stewed with salt fish or salted meat of any kind, and highly seasoned with Cayenne pepper" which he tells us was a favourite among the negro slaves. As "For bread," he continues, "an unripe roasted plantain is an excellent substitute, and universally preferred to it by the negroes, and most of the white natives."

So the Whites, noted Bryan Edwards, are no longer white, they have become natives, have become creolized.

Patrick Leigh-Fermor, in his short novel, *The Violins Of St. Jacques*, has described the social mixing of white men and women with black slaves during the Mardi Gras celebrations. It was during such an occasion that the island suffered a massive volcanic eruption and disappeared below the sea. Legend has it that whenever a boat sails over the spot, the violins can still be heard.

The African slaves, as we can see, despite their debasement as well as the debasement of their white masters, played a vital role in creolization, the creation of the Creole Society.

Mr. Edward Brathwaite notes further that, despite slavery, were "two cultures of people, having to adapt themselves to a new environment and to each other. The friction created by this confrontation was cruel, but it was also creative." Something which neither James Anthony Froude, nor Sir Vidia Naipaul refused to recognize, for no people, living through four hundred years of that of kind of existence, as was the case in the Caribbean, could do so and survive those four hundred years, without having devised certain methods, certain strategies for survival. Those methods, those strategies, whatever they were, were an integral part in the formation of the Creole Society, and of Caribbean or West Indian folk culture.

When we speak of Folk Culture, we mean the habits, customs and the ways of life of a people which they have devised in order to survive. In the context of the Caribbean, it will have to mean the culture of the mass of the black people, slaves, who had been taken to a new environment and had found ways, successfully, of adapting to that new environment.

That Folk Culture was created, and sustained by the mass of the black people who for the most part were illiterate. They did not seek the blessings, nor the approval of their white masters for that Folk Culture to be accepted and given a blessing.

Caribbean society, we have to repeat, originated in the most violent situation in modern history. The plantation system, as some social and cultural anthropologist have discovered, is indispensable for any study of Caribbean society. Indeed, it was the most important historical phenomenon to have been introduced in the Caribbean, for the Caribbean as a whole was shaped by slavery and the plantation system, and that has had a decisive influence on the formation of the culture which emerged, Creole culture.

The historical collision of races and cultures, in the beginning, Europe and Africa, produced a syncretism, a miscegenation, an acculturation, a mélange which has come to be known as Creolization; that is, a common body of historical tradition born of that historical experience which has resulted in a heterogeneous culture pattern.

In that cultural mélange, the Negro-African, as the numerically dominant group, was the principal acculturating agent in the formation of that Creole Culture. When we look at the Caribbean we recognize that, despite the mixture of races and cultures, the Negro-African contributed to an enormously significant degree to the Africanization of that Creole Culture. Jamaica, Haiti and Cuba exhibit the greatest degree of the Africanization of that culture. We have to travel to Bahia in North-Eastern Brazil for any similar manifestation.

The runaway slaves, those found principally in French Guyana, and who inhabit the dense forests, have retained their ancestral habits and their African way of life to a large extent, but they have no contact with other cultures. The Boni and the Bosche are the largest tribal groups, and they live very close to nature.

Any study of the West Indies and of the West Indians has to begin, as this book began, with a study and an examination of slavery and the Plantation System, and whatever elements of their folk culture that the Negro-Africans had brought with them and had managed to keep alive. How they survived in that new environment and under those conditions, using whatever tools that were available, and with the memories of their Negro-African traditions, helps us to establish something of their new and unique Identity. As was mentioned earlier, much of that Negro-African culture survives to this day in Haiti and amongst the Bush Negroes in the Guyanas.

There Negro-African cultural survivals, or continuum, are best found and studied for having been kept alive in those secluded communities inhabited by the runaway slaves and their descendants. Those survivals were possible, as in the case of Haiti, for example, because at the time of the Haitian Revolution and the War of Independence, some three-quarters of the slaves had been born in Africa.

In other island communities, because of their heterogeneous nature, or composition, it was not possible for the different tribal groups, or nationalities, to preserve and to maintain their traditional Negro-African cultures. In those cases the Negro-Africans had to work out their own methods of survival in that kind of environment, and to organize their communities in a way that would ensure survival. Each, in that case, contributed to that collective memory, as it were, to the whole. It was found, though, that in certain instances, in such communities, the culture of one group dominated—The Ashanti in Jamaica, the Ibo in Barbados, the Yoruba in Cuba and Trinidad, the Dahomeyan in Haiti.

Another method of survival, as has been said before, was syncretism, the identification of the Negro-African deities with the Christian God and Saints, in particular Roman Catholicism in Haiti and Brazil.

The meeting between Amerindian and Negro-African runaway slaves in Surinam and the other two Guyanas, produced another cultural syncretism, manifested in religious beliefs, and, it has also been discovered, in folklore in certain parts of Brazil.

Emancipation of the slaves came in 1834, and, to repeat, in order to stop the desertion from the plantations by the ex-slaves a system of Apprenticeship was introduced whereby the ex-slaves were tied to the plantations and were forced to work for forty-and-half hours a week for their former masters without pay. Even children were compulsorily apprenticed.

The experiences of the ex-slaves under the Apprenticeship System were no different than they had been under slavery, so they rebelled and deserted the plantations in large numbers. There were periodic marches and demonstrations in the streets and the planters were forced to abolish the Apprenticeship System three years earlier than had been scheduled. That brought on a serious problem of labour on the plantations and the planters were forced to look elsewhere for labour for the ex-slaves refused to remain on the estates unless they received better wages which the planters refused to do.

The Planters first sought Portuguese labour from Madeira, but they died in large numbers of various diseases and from the exacting work on the plantations. The planters, therefore, either had to pay the ex-slaves new and better wages, or close down the plantations and the sugar factories. They decided, instead, to import Asiatics from India, China and Java. The contract was the same as it had been for the indentured labourers who had come, for the most part, from Ireland.

The first Indian indentured labourers arrived in the West Indies on two vessels, the *Whitby* and the *Hesperus*, on the 5th. May, 1838, the year in which the Apprenticeship System ended in the British West Indies. On board the two vessels were a total of 396 men, women and children.

The new arrivals were treated as badly as had been the Negro-African slaves. They endured every form of cruelty and lived in houses under the most degrading of conditions. The importation of the Asiatics to replace the ex-slaves was meant, also, to create competition for employment. It had been meant as a strategy to get the ex-slaves to return to the plantations and the estates at very meagre wages.

The importation of Asiatics lasted for some seventy-five years. Their places of abode were more like cattle pens, although they were called barracks. Those indentured Asiatics were whipped and were subject to the same slave laws for absenteeism; wages were meagre and were subject to stoppages and even, on occasions, withheld for several years. Or, invariably, they had pay for two days deducted whenever anyone was absent for a day, or an extra day was added to their period of indenture for every day absent.

The system came to an end in 1917, due primarily to the political agitation of Mahatma Ghandi who had campaigned against the treatment and condition of Indians in the Fiji Islands in the Pacific and which had aroused public opinion in India.

The indentured labourers went mainly to the British Caribbean islands, in particular Trinidad and Guyana, and to a lesser extent to the Windward Islands, including Saint Lucia, where there still remain large numbers of Indians. The period of indenture was between five and seven years and, as has been mentioned above, and as Father Labat had discovered about the Irish indentured labourers in Barbados, every excuse was found to extend that period.

The Asiatics came with their distinct cultural traits — language, religion, beliefs and practices and marriage customs. They introduced certain elements of their culture, in particular, their cuisine, music, theatre and shops; the Chinese went into the laundry business and introduced gambling which seems to have been a national past-time in China. In time they added to the mixture of races, and in Jamaica where the creator of the James Bond character was created by Ian Fleming, the mixture of Chinese and Negro-African was known as 'Chingroes,' and in Saint Lucia, the mixture of Indian and Negro-African were called by the Creole word, 'douglas.'

It has been observed by social and cultural anthropologists that where different racial groups inhabit the same communities, it is almost impossible for each society, each racial group to exist without the sharing of values common to all, of borrowings one from the other of certain cultural elements. Even where, as in Trinidad and Guyana, for example, with Hindus and Moslems, certain values, those relating to marriage and family life, differ from those of the Negro-Africans, it was necessary that there should be an integration of the components of units which would constitute a common set of values in order to achieve unity in the society.

That unity is imperative for the pursuit of particular goals. All members of the society, regardless of ethnic differences, must obey those rules and the laws; what some sociologists call 'Willing Submission.' Otherwise the alternative is utter chaos, total anarchy.

That was the tragedy on the Indian sub-continent after the granting of Independence and which resulted in the creation of separate states—India, Pakistan, Bangladesh. The unity of the society, previously, had been based on force exercised by the colonial rulers, England, and when these Imperialists departed, everything turned 'ole mas' as the Trinidadians say. The cleavages and the slaughter which erupted were of horrifying proportions. The theory of subordination and identification could not hold, and what followed were segmented loyalties; there existed no common values.

In the Caribbean those common values had been imposed and upheld by the dominance of the colonial powers who shared those common values and which they used to dominate and control the slaves by forceful regulations — Slave Laws in the Spanish Caribbean, Police regulations in the British West Indies, and the Code Noir in the French Antilles. Planter interests had to be maintained and protected at all costs.

Military force, as we have seen, was also present and was used in the Caribbean to maintain that slave system which remained in existence till the abolition of slavery between 1834 in the British West Indies and 1848 in the French Antilles. After that some measure of functional coherence introduced stability, despite the multi-ethnic nature of the society.

Later in the twentieth century regional organizations such as the Organization of Eastern Caribbean States, and the larger CARICOM (Caribbean Community) were established. In the latter, both the independent states of the former colonial territories as well as Haiti and Surinam are full members, with the Dominican Republic and Venezuela having Observer status. The organizations are a sort of Pan-Caribbeanness which is meant to work towards and to establish a common ideal — the Caribbean Personality.

As has been observed there is no single definition of Culture. Some cultural anthropologists, M. G. Smith being one, describe Culture as a "complex whole which includes knowledge, beliefs, art, laws, morals, customs and any other capabilities and habits acquired by man as a member of society." Others define Culture as a "product; is historical; it includes ideas, patterns, and values; is selective; is learned; is based upon symbols; and is an abstraction from behaviour and the products of behaviour."

In Haiti, the work of Dr. Jean Price-Mars was a catalyst for the nationalist movement which eventually forced the North Americans to leave the occupation of their country. In other colonial territories Culture was used to justify demands for Independence by stressing the cultural difference and distinctiveness of the particular territories, as in Kenya, India, Senegal, Guinea and Algeria, for example. In Algeria, as Franz Fanon revealed in *The Wretched Of The Earth*, culture distinctiveness was used to promote political unity and to legitimize the people's political movement.

This question is often asked: Have the West Indies a separate culture? Are they a homogeneous nation?

To the first question the answer has to be in the affirmative, with some qualifications due to the historical experiences of the different territories and the particular method of administration by the colonial powers — French, Spanish, Dutch and British.

To the second the answer has to be in the negative for, as Sir Shridath Ramphal has pointed out, the West Indies, a region of just over six million inhabitants, comprises some sixteen sovereign countries and has the world's highest density of government anywhere on this planet, Earth, and is the world's most intensely bureaucratized and the most politicised region found anywhere in this world.

In George Lamming's second novel, *The Emigrants*, a character, Tornado, we will recall on the boat during the voyage of the emigrants to England, musing on the situation in the West Indies, is perhaps thinking of the future of possibilities when he says to an assembled company "We got to suffer first and then come together. If there's one thing England going to teach all 'o we is that there ain't no place like home no matter how bad home is. But you got to pay to learn, an' believe me I may not see it but those comin' after goin' make better West Indian men for comin' up here an' seein' for themselves what is what." A Jamaican, also addressing the gathering on the boat, says :

> "Doctor, nurse, lawyer, engineer, commercial man, woman and man, them all that study an' call themselves West Indies people as though them was a completely new generation or race the Almighty Gawd create yesterday, them all want to prove somethin', an' them sensitive, them 'fraid, 'cause them ain't want the foreign man to feel that them ain't proving....Them want to prove that them is themselves ... We never hear so much talk lately 'bout West Indies. Everybody sayin' me is West Indian. We is West Indians. West Indian this, West Indian that."

THE FINAL PATTERN

About two decades ago the *CARICOM* Heads of Government set up what was called 'The West Indies Commission,' which had as its Chairman, Sir Shridath Ramphal. The Commissioners travelled to every territory in the former British colonial territories, interviewing people, politicians, and organizations. The objective was to find out the views of the people of the region on the possibility of further integration into a larger single nation and the people's response to the opportunities and challenges of the time and of the future. Quoting some lines from Derek Walcott's *Omeros*, Sir Shridath Ramphal began his report saying:

> *"The fluent culture of time has already changed us; we the diverse people of scattered islands and mainland countries plucked from far continents by cruel history, drawing strength from our variety of race and culture and place of origin, but reaching beyond them for other strengths from uniting elements. Historical forces and the Caribbean Sea have divided us; yet unfolding history and that same sea, through long centuries of struggle against uneven odds, have been steadily making us one. Now West Indians have emerged with an identity clearly recognisable not only to ourselves and our wider Caribbean but also in the world beyond the Caribbean Sea."*

Sir Shridath Ramphal is of Indian descent, but he reminded his audience that "I am Guyanese before I am Indian; I am a West Indian before I am a Guyanese." Oneness, he says "has replaced separateness in four generations. So it is for most of the people of our Caricom Region. That oneness is the basic reality of our West Indian condition."

Several centuries before him, the French Jesuit priest, Father Jean-Baptiste Labat, had set out as far back as the end of the eighteenth century, the hypothesis for a Caribbean Culture, and that Culture, he observed, was being expressed through Music, Song, Dance and Rhythm, the linguistic and political frontiers imposed by the various European powers notwithstanding:

> *"I have travelled everywhere in your sea of the Caribbean, from Haiti to Barbados, to Martinique and Guadeloupe, and I know what I am speaking about. You are together, in the same boat, sailing on the same uncertain sea, citizenship and race*

unimportant, feeble little labels compared to the message that my spirit brings to me: that of the position and predicament which History has imposed upon you."

Father Labat ends "It is no accident that the sea which separates your lands makes no difference to the rhythm of your body."

West Indians of late years have become aware that they and their culture are distinct and different from other peoples and other countries, but they also recognise the cultural diversity in the various islands — French, Dutch, Spanish, British. Those differences, as we have seen, have been due to the different historical and metropolitan administrations and affiliations.

As Father Labat had prophesised, despite those historical affiliations, the sea that divides the islands makes no difference, but, rather, offers, or points to a future of possibilities. The people are now all Creoles and that Creole Culture had its basis in slavery, the plantation system, indentured labour and colonialism. The institutions were imposed by Europe — Government, Religion, Education, Law — but those institutions differ in several particulars from the metropolitan models and were fashioned, or rather, re-fashioned to fit local conditions, aspirations such as moral values, habits, customs and patterns of behaviour.

Those who came later and have settled in the West Indies have adopted the way of life of the Creoles, and have themselves become creolized. Plantation life and plantation society required certain adaptations which brought into being that distinct Creole Culture. Racial mixtures, as we have seen, and as treated in the book, *Children Of Caliban*, by Fernando Henriques, added to the picture of Creole Society and Creole Culture. The lifestyles of the Creoles governed the accommodation of the new arrivals from Asia, and, even where some groups tried to keep themselves ethnically separate, or isolated, they soon found that in order to survive and to participate in the activities in their new environment — Steelband, Calypso, Carnival — all had gradually to become what the people of Martinique and Guadeloupe call 'Creolité.'

Where there has been racial conflict of very recent times, in Guyana, that conflict, as the late Dr. Jedi Chagan, one-time Prime Minister had pointed out in his book *The West On Trial*, had been fermented by political and economic interests in the USA and Great Britain, when it was thought that an independent Guyana under Dr.

Jagan, would follow the political, social and economic routes that Cuba under President Fidel Castro, had established.

Creole Society, as has been mentioned, was one with "some unusual characteristics," says Franklin W. Knight in his book, *The Caribbean*, and he points out that the Negro-African slaves could not "maintain their demographic viability as other social units did in Africa, Europe and within the indigenous Amerindian communities."

The slave society was, as he said "predominantly male, predominantly adult, predominantly non-free, and relentlessly coerced." Nevertheless, it would be wrong", Dr. Knight continues, to "assert that these societies were not dynamic, resilient, creative, and strong."

Masters and slaves were inter-dependent and the society which emerged was not created by any one single racial group. "Masters and slaves," says Dr. Knight, "did not, could not, form two totally independent communities." Both masters and slaves, and time, created that Creole Society, those Creole traditions which eventually came into existence.

That Creolization, which had started with the Blacks, the Whites and the Mulattos, is now virtually complete.

Daniel Cowley, in his contribution 'Cultural Assimilation in a Multiracial Society' (*West Indian Perspectives* edited by Lambros Comitas and David Lowenthal), notes that:

> *"Unconscious assimilation is a much more subtle process and, like culture itself, not often perceived by its practitioners. Through this process West Indian-born Whites are no longer Englishmen or Frenchmen and never fully belong to their ancestral cultures. The same process works for the Chinese, Syrians, Portuguese, and other groups who preserve some aspects of their ancestral traditions, but otherwise belong to the local culture more than they realize."*

That only serves to remind us that when peoples of different cultures meet in large numbers in a particular environment, their original cultures become altered, for culture is dynamic, constantly changing and is never static, even in the most conservative of societies. However powerful or determined are the efforts to retain and preserve the original culture, such efforts can never succeed. The peoples, when they meet, and as they interact with each other, borrow elements of each other's culture and, in the course of time, those borrowed elements combine with the original cultures, and something new in terms of forms, customs, beliefs and values, comes into existence.

When Europe, Africa, India and China met in the West Indies, and the borrowings took place, a new culture emerged, worked out by the descendants of the peoples of those four continents who were born and raised in the Region — Creole Culture. That new culture was nothing resembling the original cultures with which each had arrived in the Caribbean. Those peoples inevitably have had to interact and to associate with each other on a daily basis in the shops, markets, fields, and in village life in general as Samuel Selvon has dramatized in his novel, *Turn Again Tiger*. Creolization of all the ethnic groups became inevitable.

There are other powerful influences, also, which go to work in the process of that Creolization — Schools, libraries, books, newspapers, religion, even; Sports such as Cricket, Carnival, Calypso, the Steelband, Radio and Television—all are potent sources of the unconscious assimilation and the Creolization of which Professor Cowley spoke.

To-day in the West Indies and the wider Caribbean, a new order is being worked out, a common set of values specifically and uniquely Caribbean. A Nigerian writer, Kole Omotosi, says that no one ought to:

> *"generalise about any issue relating to the Caribbean. This is not because of any incomprehensible complexity. Rather, the situation of the Caribbean is like a kaleidoscope where new colours and new colour combinations keep turning up. There are still so many unknowns, so many unmentionables, too many prickly facts and information which lie buried in the past. The more that past becomes generally available, acceptable and undistorted, the better for the future of Caribbean Studies."*

It was the late C. L. R. James who noted that the West Indians are a people unique in the modern world and that there has never been any people like them, both positively and negatively in the recorded history of mankind. Any study of them is therefore a tremendous undertaking.

What of the future of the West Indies? What contributions can the West Indians make to world culture and civilization?

The West Indies and the West Indians inhabit a world to-day that is becoming increasingly inter-dependent. It is a world, also, in which advancing technology has revealed man's capacity for self-destruction. It will be a world of giant states such as India and China. If man is to survive on this planet, Earth, then there must be methods and strategies put in place urgently to allow for greater cooperation amongst the nations and peoples of the world, for never in the history of mankind has there been a greater need of each other for the nations and peoples of the world and, above all, for the acknowledgement and respect for the dignity of human beings.

The peoples of the world, in order to survive, as the masters and slaves and their descendants had realized in the Caribbean and had worked out for themselves, have to work out a basis for co-existence.

Aimé Césaire had insisted on reminding the world that, as West Indians, we know that there is still work to be done, that no race possesses a monopoly of beauty, of intelligence, of force, and that there is a place for all at the rendezvous of victory — the victory of human dignity.

Decades after Césaire had made that declaration of supreme optimism, another West Indian, the Nobel Prize Winner, Sir Arthur Lewis, addressing students at a graduation ceremony at the Barbados Campus of the University of the West Indies, reminded West Indians that they must strive to be themselves, and not Africans, Frenchmen, Indians or Chinese. "Societies differ," he said, "not in the underlying humanity, but in what they make of themselves and of their environment. What differs is the human achievement," and that West Indians "must make something different — our achievement must be unique."

Those achievements and that uniqueness are to be found in West Indian literature, art, music, dance and a distinct way of life. That will be the West Indian contribution to world culture and civilization.

BIBLIOGRAPHY

Baldwin, Jones, *Notes Of A Native Son*
Bascomb, William, *Shango In the new World*
Bastide, Roger, *African Civilizations in The New World*
Brathwaite, Edward, *The Development of Creole Society In Jamaica, 1770—1820*
Babinais, Le Gentil de la, *Nouveau Voyage Autour de Monde*
Boxer, C. L., *The Colour Question in the Portuguese Empire 1415-1825*
Benitez-Rojo, Antonio *The Repeating Island*
Césaire, Aime, *Cahier D'Un Retour Au Pays Natal*
  – *Discours sur le Colonialisme*
Comias, Lambros, *West Indian Perspectives*
Deren, Maya, *The Divine Horsemen*
Dunn, Richard, *Sugar and Slaves*
Edwards, Bryan, *A History, Civil & Commercial Of the British West Indies*
Elder, J.D., *The Yoruba Ancestor Cult in Gasparillo*
Freyre, Giberto, *Masters and Slaves*
Froude, James, Anthony, *The English In The West Indies*
Garvey, Marcus, *The Philosophy and Opinions of*
Goveia, Elsa, *The West Indian Slave Laws*
  – S*lave Society in the British Leeward Islands At The End Of The Eighteenth Century*
  – *A Study on the Histiography of the British West Indies*
Hegel, G. W. F., *The Philosophy of History*
Heller, Eric, *The Disinherited Mind*
Herskovits, M.J., *The Myth of the Negro Past*
  – *Life in a Haitian Village*
James, C. L. R.,*The Black Jacobins*
  – *Beyond A Boundary*
  – *A History of Negro Revolt*
Jahn, Jnheinz, *Muntu*
  – *A History of Neo-African Literature*
Johnson, DeGraft, *African Glory*
Knight, Franklin, *The Caribbean*
Kestleloot, Lilyan, *Les ecrivains noir de langue francaise: naissance d'un literature*
Leyburn, James ,*The Haitian People*

Labat, Père, *The Memoirs of*
Lamming, George, *In The Castle Of My Skin*
 – *The Emigrants*
 – *Of Age And Innocence*
 – *Season of Adventure*
 – *The Pleasures of Exile*
Lowenthal, David, (Ed.)*West Indian Perspectives*
Lewis, Sir Arthur, *On Being Different*
Memmi, Albert,*The Colonizer and The Colonized*
Mannoni, O., *Prospero and Caliban – The Psychology of Colonization*
Malone, Thomas, *De La Negritude Dans la Literature Negro-Africaine*
Marsh, Henry, *Slavery And Race – The Story Of Slavery and Its Legacy*
Nath, Dwaka, *A History of Indians in Guyana*
Padmore, George, *Africa, Britain's Third Empire*
 – *Pan-Africanism or Communism*
Price-Mars, Jean *Ainsi Parla L' Oncle*
 – *De Saint-Dominique à Haiti*
Reid, Vic, *New Day*
Rigo, Milo, *Le Tradition Voodoo Et le Voodoo Haitien*
St. Mery, Moreau de, *Description topographique, physique, etc. de l'isle Saint-Dominique*
Sarte, Jean-Paul, *Orphée Noir*
Senghor, Sedar, Leopold, *Négritude et Humanisme*
 –*Negritude et Civilisation de 'L'Universelle'*
Schmidt, Hans, *The United States Occupation of Haiti 1913-1934*
Spendler, Oswald, *The Decline of the West*
Smith M. G., *The Plural Society in the British West Indies*
Thomas, John, Jacob, *Froudacity*
Walcott, Derek, *In A Green Night*
 – *Castaway*
 – *Another life*
 – *The Antilles, Fragments of Epic Memory*
 – *What The Twilight Says*

INDEX

Atlantic Charter, 59
Atlee, Clement, 59

Black Jacobins, The, C.L.R. James, 15,16, 47
Blackstone, Sir William, 21
Barbados, Slave uprising in, 30, 31, 32
Breton, Andre, 71, 77
Brathwaite, Edward 93,155,156,161,162,166
Bernard, Regnor, 118
Bascom, William *Shango in the New World*, 146
Bastide, R, *African Civilizations in the New World*, 146
Benitez-Rojo, Antonio, *The Repeating Island*, 162

Cesaire, Aime, 14,15,71,73,76,78,92 160
Creation of Caribbean Society, 19
Coartacion, 20
Code Noir, 24, 25, 26, 27, 28
Churches and the Clergy, The Established, 40, 41
Chagaramas, 61,62
Churchill, Sir Winston, 59, 60
Cahier D'Un Retour Au Pays Natal, 71- 81
Cathcart, Colonel, 99
De Charlevoix, Pierre Francois, 146
Creole and Creolization, 161,162,165,166
Cultural Assimilation in a

Multiracial Society (from *West Indian Perspectives*) David Cowley, 175

Deren, Maya, *The Divine Horsemen*, 147
Desasalines, 55, 99
Diop, David, *Poems*, 151
Diop, Alioune, 37
Desportes, George, 72
DuBoulay, Count, 44
Dominion Status, 50
Durham Report re Dominion Status, 50
Durand, Oswald, 74

Eannes de Azuzara, Gomes, *The Chronicle of the Discovery And Conquest of Guinea*, 11, 12
Effects of Culture Contacts, 11
Europe in present day West Indian life, 11
English Law regarding private property, 20, 21, 25
Economic activities of the slaves, 23
Edwards, Bryan, *History, Civil and Commercial, Of the British Colonies in the West Indies*, 24, 42, 44,166
East, (India and China), The Introduction of the, 67
Eboue, Felix, 78
Elder, Dr. J. D., *The Yoruba Ancestral Cult in Gasparillo*, 186

INDEX

Fanon, Franz, *The Wretched of the Earth*, 84, 172
Freyre, Gilberto, *The Masters and the Slaves – A Study In the Development of Brazilian Civilization*, 9, 10
French West Indies, 24,25
Frobenius, Leo, 71
Froude, James Anthony, *The Bow of Ulysses*, 83, 95, 96, 97, 98

Garvey, Marcus, 105, 106
Guillen, Nicholas, *Poems*, 37, 69, 93,114
Gentil de la Babinais, 44
Goveia, Elsa, *Slave Society in the British Leeward Islands At the End of the Eighteenth Century*; *The West Indian Slave Laws of the Eighteenth Century*, 52
Guberina, Peter, 81, 86,

Haklyut, 13
Hawkins, Sir John, 13
Hegel, W.G., 79
Heller, Eric, 69, 70
Henriques, Fernando, *Children of Caliban*, 174
Herskovits, Melville, The Myth of the Negro Past, 9
Homer, *The Iliad*, 154

Idowu, Dr. E. Bolaji, *Olodumare – God in Yoruba Belief*, 148
–Ill-treatment of Slaves in the British West Indies, 24, 25

Jagan, Dr. Chedi, *The West On Trial*, 174, 175
James, C. L. R., *The Black Jacobins, Beyond a Boundary, Party Politics in the West Indies,* 15, 16, 28, 31, 36, 47, 49,52, 53, 54, 56,57,62, 63, 100, 109,112, 155, 156
Jahn, Janheinz, Muntu, *The History of Neo-African Literature*, 78

Kestleloot, Mademe Lilyn, *Les ecrivains noirs de langue francaise, Naissance d'une litterature,* 78
Knight, Dr. Franklin, *The Caribbean*, 175

Labat, Jean Baptiste Father, 32, 33, 34, 173, 174
Laleau, Leon, 115
Lamming, George, 65, 67, 127-141, 143, 154, 155, 159, 172
Leclerc, General, 55, 57
Lewis, Dr. Arthur, *On Being Different,* 177
Ligon, Richard, *A True and Exact History of the Island of Barbados*,15, 16, 30, 31, 32, 34, 40, 45, 66, 163,164
Lowenthal, David, *West Indian Societies*, 165

Makandal, 47, 48
McKay, Claude, *Poems*, 70, 115
Macaulay, Lord, *Lays of Ancient Rome*, 153, 154
Mansfield, Lord Chief Justice, 21, 22

Mannoni, *Psychology of Colonization*, 79
Marcelin, Philippe Thoby, 71, 72, 74,
Maran, Rene, *Batouala*, 10, 78, 118, 119
Marriage and Concubinage, 66, 67
Mau Mau uprising, 73
Melone, Thomas, *De la negritude dans la literature africaine*, 78
Meni, Albert, *The Colonizer and the Colonized*, 79
Music in religious rites, 11

Olney, Richard, 102, 103
Omotosi, Kole, *The Theatrical into Theatre*, 176

Padmore, George, 60, 61, 106, 107, 108, 110,
Pares, Richard, *Mercahdn and Plamnters*, *War and Trade In the West Indies*, 39, 45, 59
Phenomenon of possession, 11
Police Force, 16, 25
Police Regulations, 22, 23, 25, 29
Political structure, 11, 38, 39
Price-Mars, Dr. Jean, 94, 98, 101, 102, 103, 104, 105

Ramphal, Shridath, *Inseperable Humanity*, 172, 173
Raynal, Abbe, 46, 47
Restrictions on Slave Activities, 23
Reid, Vic, *New Day*, *The Leopard*, 119-124
Rodman, Selden, 101, 102
Royal Navy, Role of, 16, 25

Roumain, Jacques, 41, 71, 72, 73

Siete Partidas, 19, 20,
Spanish Slave Laws, 19
St. Mery, Moreau, 28, 49
Stowell, Judge, 28
Status of children under le Code Noir, 26
Social Structure, The, 41, 42
De Stael, Madame, 36
Smith, Adam, *The Wealth of Nations*, 21, 46, 51, 52, 59, 100
Spengler, Oswald, *The Decline of the West*, 69, 70
Senghor, Leopol Sedar, Poems, *Negritude et Humanism*, 75, 76, 81, 82
Sartre, Jean-Paul, *Black Orpheus*, 76, 77
Syncretism, 168

Trial by Jury, 23, 24, 26
Thackeray, W, *Vanity Fair*, 36
Toussaingt L'Ouverture's Letter to Napoleon Bonaparte, 52
Tirolien, Guy, 72, 73, 74, 75, 116
Trilling, Lionel, 69
Thomas, John Jacob, *The Theory and Practice of Creole Grammar – Froudacity*, 95, 96, 97
Tempels, Father Placide, *La Philosophie Bantu*, 168

Vanity Fair, by William Thackeray, 43, 145
Voodoo, 151-153

Williams, Dr. Eric, *Capitalism*

and Slavery, From Columbus To Castro, 28, 36, 37, 52, 61,
Wordsworth, William, *Toussaint L'Ouverture*, 54, 55
Wilberforce, William, 51, 52
Waller, John, 42
Williams, Dennis, *Other Leopards*, 124 -126
Walcott, Derek, 115, 149